CRITICAL THINKING

FOR SQA HIGHER & INTERMEDIATE 2 PHILOSOPHY

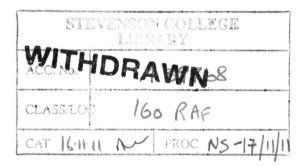
John Rafferty

Kynoch & Blaney

Kynoch & Blaney Limited
Registered Office: Sherwood House, 7 Glasgow Road, Paisley PA1 3QS.

First published 2007.

British Library Cataloguing in Publication Data
A catalogue record for this book can be obtained from the British Library.

ISBN-13 digit: 978-0-9553973-1-8
ISBN-10 digit: 0-9553973-1-6

Text formatting designed by Kynoch & Blaney Ltd.

Cover photograph by Jastrow (2006) of the Roman copy of Lysippus' bust of Aristotle after a Greek bronze original from 330 BC. From the Ludovisi Collection, Museo Nazionale Romano, Rome, Italy. Accessed from Wikipedia and copyright free under the following statement: *'I, the copyright holder of this work, hereby release it into the public domain. This applies worldwide.'*

Cover concept and design by Kynoch & Blaney and Douglas McLeod, DAM Design, Glasgow.

Printed and bound by Bell and Bain Ltd., Glasgow, UK.

What Others Have Said about this Book

Colin Price, SQA Principal Assessor for Philosophy and Principal Teacher of Religious, Moral and Philosophical Studies, The High School of Glasgow:

"Although there are other books on logic and critical thinking, this book is, as far as I know, the only one currently written specifically for the SQA's units on 'Critical Thinking in Philosophy.' In doing this John has performed a great service for those lecturers and teachers trying to resource their courses. John Rafferty has the knack of taking what can be for some students a difficult topic and explaining it in a clear and easily understood way. The many exercises will not only help the busy teacher but will be invaluable to the student, for this is a book that is intended to be used and not just read."

Jane Henderson, Senior Lecturer in Communication and Core Skills, James Watt College of Further and Higher Education:

"Lucid, thorough and engaging, this book is an ideal introductory text for Critical Thinking in the Scottish curriculum. Students will particularly appreciate the activities, with answers, which carefully guide the reader from chapter to chapter. It deserves, moreover, a wider readership: any student of law, social sciences or media will find that it sharpens the ear for poor reasoning, while members of the public interested in clear thinking will like-wise find it a stimulating read."

Jim Carmichael, Lecturer in Philosophy, Anniesland College, Glasgow:

"John Rafferty has produced with his text, Critical Thinking for SQA Higher & Intermediate 2 Philosophy (2007), *just exactly what students and teachers working on Higher and Intermediate courses need. It is a text that neither assumes too much nor asks too much, but is pitched at that important developmental level where there has been such a gap in published material for so long in Scotland. The text takes students through quite complex philosophical points concerning the nature and mechanics of argument and introduces them to fallacies in their various manifestations. Importantly, John Rafferty has also provided the reader with a whole variety of activities and exercises which stimulate thinking and give students the opportunity to learn through doing.* Critical Thinking for SQA Higher & Intermediate 2 Philosophy (2007) *is an invaluable addition to the resources available for learning and teaching Philosophy in Scotland."*

Acknowledgements

I would firstly like to acknowledge all at Kynoch & Blaney for their indefatigable enthusiasm and professionalism during the production of this text. I would also like to thank Colin Price (*The High School of Glasgow*), Jim Carmichael (*Anniesland College*) and Jane Henderson (*James Watt College*) for their kind comments. A special thank you goes to my esteemed colleagues at Langside College Glasgow and at the SQA for their positive and good-humoured support, particularly the Philosophy marking team from whom I have learned a great deal: some of it even relevant to Philosophy.

I would also like to thank Jastow for making his image of Lysippus' bust of Aristotle available copyright free on *Wikipedia*, and Douglas McLeod of DAM Design, Glasgow for excellent work on the cover.

Last, but by no means least, I would like to thank Fiona for making the writing of this book at all possible and I would like to dedicate this book to our daughter Kate, the most critical thinker I know.

Contents

Chapter 6 Fallacies

Chapter 7 Study and Revision Guide

Glossary of Key Terms

Index

Introduction

Who is this Book for?

This Book is for students and teachers of introductory critical thinking courses. The motivation behind writing this book arose from a number of misgivings about existing texts. First, was the observation that many books on critical thinking and logic very often go far beyond the needs of most students. This has the effect of frightening off students who are startled by chapters on 'advanced predicate calculus' when their course requires much less. Second, was the fact that so many books are aimed at an undergraduate university audience and so are rarely written in plain and simple language with practice exercises and comprehensive sets of answers. Finally, there is also a dearth of materials written specifically for the Scottish curriculum. This leaves teachers and students to cobble together an understanding of the subject from a variety of sources, which can be an expensive and time-consuming task. It is therefore hoped that this Book goes some way to addressing these concerns.

This Book is therefore primarily designed with the SQA Higher and Intermediate 2 Philosophy units in Critical Thinking in mind and the required content of both these units is fully addressed by the chapters within. It is hoped that it is comprehensive enough in terms on content, exercises and feedback to function as a stand alone text for use by students or teachers of critical thinking; either to support conventional classroom delivery, or as a required text in open or distance learning contexts. This book would also make an excellent basic introduction to Critical Thinking or Logic for other certificated or non-certificated courses by other institutions or awarding bodies out with Scotland.

Critical Thinking in the Scottish Curriculum

In the Scottish curriculum, Critical Thinking is a component of both the SQA Higher Philosophy course (C237 12) and the Intermediate 2 Philosophy course (C237 11). The Higher unit, Critical Thinking (DV55 12), is broader in scope than the Intermediate 2 unit, Critical Thinking (DV55 11), and has some additional content. This is reflected in both the unit and course assessments for these units which offer contrasting levels of difficulty.

Intermediate 2 Unit Outcomes

Intermediate 2 Critical Thinking assesses only **two** Outcomes, requiring students to:

a) Demonstrate an understanding of the building blocks of arguments.
    a. Describe the difference between statements and arguments.
    b. Use ordinary language examples to support this description.
    c. Given previously unseen examples of ordinary language arguments, identify their premises and conclusions.

b) Critically examine ordinary language arguments.
    a. Given previously unseen examples of ordinary language argument, present the premises and conclusions in a structured manner.
    b. Explain specific examples of unreliable reasoning.
    c. Explain whether or not the conclusions follow from true premises.
    d. State reasons to support the explanations given.

Higher Unit Outcomes

Higher Critical Thinking assesses **three** Outcomes, requiring students to:

1. Demonstrate an understanding of the nature of arguments.
    a. Describe the difference between statements and arguments.
    b. Describe the difference between deductive and inductive reasoning.
    c. Use ordinary language examples to support these descriptions.

2. Critically analyse ordinary language arguments.
    a. Identify the premises and conclusions of ordinary language arguments.
    b. Present these arguments in a way which demonstrates the stages of reasoning involved.
    c. Explain whether these arguments employ deductive or inductive reasoning.

3. Critically evaluate ordinary language arguments.
    a. Explain specific examples of fallacious reasoning in ordinary language arguments.
    b. Explain whether or not the conclusions of these arguments follow from the premises.
    c. Explain whether these arguments are sound or unsound.
    d. State reasons which support the explanations given.

How to use this Book

The chapters in this Book are designed to develop knowledge of the subject incrementally. The concepts introduced in Chapter 1 are therefore a necessary prerequisite for Chapter 2 and so on. Critical thinking is similar to mathematics in this respect: a grasp of fundamental concepts are required before more complex ideas can be understood. It is therefore advised that the material is tackled in the sequential order in which it has been presented.

Critical thinking is also a subject that requires practice to master. It is crucial that students new to the subject are familiar with more than one or two examples to fully grasp how each concept functions in a variety of contexts. The exercises provided at the end of each chapter must therefore be regarded as essential tasks that need to be tackled before moving on to the next chapter. Subsequent chapters have been written on the assumption that the previous concepts have been not only covered but mastered.

Critical thinking is unavoidably a subject that contains a number of technical terms. Throughout this book the key terms have been **emboldened** to draw them to your attention. Definitions of these words can be found in the glossary of key terms located at the end of the book.

About the Author

John Rafferty is a Senior Lecturer in Philosophy at Langside College, Glasgow. He holds degrees in philosophy, management and education from the University of Glasgow, Glasgow Caledonian University and the University of Strathclyde. He has taught philosophy, logic and critical thinking for the last 14 years at NQ, HND and A level. John also has 10 years experience working as an educational consultant: designing, assessing, verifying and supporting philosophy courses on behalf of the Scottish Qualifications Authority (SQA), the Higher Still Development Unit (HSDU), the Scottish Further Education Unit (SFEU), the Colleges' Open Learning Exchange Group (Coleg), the University of Strathclyde, the Scottish Executive and a variety of schools and local education authorities across Scotland. Previous publications include the nationally published support materials *Logic* (Coleg, 2000); *Classic Texts in Philosophy* (Coleg, 2001); *Problems in Philosophy* (Coleg, 2002); *Higher Moral Philosophy* (SFEU, 2006); *Intermediate 2 Moral Philosophy* (SFEU, 2006); *Evaluating Philosophical Issues in the Social Sciences* (Coleg, 2007); *An Introduction to Analytic Philosophy* (Coleg, 2007) as well a number of magazine articles.

Chapter 1

What is Critical Thinking?

What does Critical Thinking Involve?

Critical thinking is a term that has gained widespread use in recent years in schools, colleges and universities. Examination authorities have introduced new courses in critical thinking throughout the UK and most educational sectors now see it as a key skill essential to success in Higher Education, as important as essay writing or exam technique. However, it is also a term that is used to refer a number of quite distinct activities, so it is worth spending some time defining what this subject involves.

In everyday life we use arguments all the time when discussing an infinite variety of issues. We argue about football, politics, religion, music and art. We also argue about trivial matters like who should pay the bills and whose turn it is to put the cat out at night. Regardless of what an argument is about though, there are common features that all successful arguments share. Critical thinking is the art of analysing and evaluating such arguments to assess how reliably they support their conclusions. It is about developing the skill of constructing effective arguments and avoiding the most common errors that people make when they argue.

In evaluating arguments we need to critically assess them in a number of different ways. This will involve:

- Identifying the relevant parts of the argument.
- Locating the premises and conclusions of the argument.
- Making any 'hidden' premises explicit.
- Examining these statements and assessing their truth or falsity.
- Clarifying the structure of the argument.
- Evaluating the argument's validity and soundness.
- Exposing any fallacies contained within the argument.

Don't worry if this list involves words or concepts you aren't familiar with. The purpose of this book is to teach you about all the relevant concepts for critical thinking and to develop a basic degree of proficiency in assessing arguments.

Why Study Critical Thinking?

Many people first encounter critical thinking as a component of philosophy courses in schools, college and universities where it is related to the study of **logic**. This is because philosophy, unlike biology or chemistry, is all about *arguments* rather than *facts*. Critical thinking therefore teaches the essential skills required in order to do philosophy properly. Before we can argue over questions like 'Are human beings free?' or 'Could our entire life be a dream?' we need to know what an argument is and know how to distinguish good arguments from bad ones. So, studying critical thinking will make you a better philosopher.

The prevalence of critical thinking in philosophy courses stems from the fact that critical thinking owes its origins to early philosophers. Over 2000 years ago, **Aristotle** (384-322 BC) wrote some of the earliest surviving texts on critical thinking and argument technique, which he called **organon** (meaning 'tool' or 'instrument'), because he felt that this subject was a necessary instrument for the pursuit of philosophy. Part of his method involved the use of special three-line arguments called **syllogisms,** which helped clarify the steps in his reasoning. Syllogisms are always three lines long and the first two lines (known as the **premises**) always entail the third (known as the **conclusion**). An example of an Aristotelian syllogism might therefore be:

- All men are mortal
  No gods are mortal
  Therefore, no men are gods

However, for Aristotle, critical thinking wasn't simply an instrument for use in philosophy alone, but was a tool to be applied in every sort of academic and practical endeavour, including psychology, biology, physics and ethics.

This fact remains true today and indeed many students might study critical thinking out with philosophy altogether. The ability to analyse texts, to extract and evaluate the arguments within them, is one of the central building blocks of becoming an independent learner in the study of any subject. Furthermore, critical thinking is now recognised as a transferable skill in its own right, of crucial importance in a host of different professions. Politics, journalism, law and management all demand the ability to take a position with regard to an issue and to defend it successfully. Moreover, given that powerful political and commercial interests spend large sums of money trying to sway our opinions, the ability to objectively scrutinise the political arguments of the day is essential in being an effective participant in a modern democracy.

Critical Thinking versus Logic

Given that logic courses and critical thinking courses both involve the study of arguments, what is the difference between these two disciplines? The short answer is that critical thinking and logic are very closely related. The main difference is really one of degree: critical thinking is the *informal* study of arguments while logic pursues a more *formal* approach.

Logic aims at capturing the underlying structure of an argument by using a formal notation: letters and symbols that represent the words and sentences in the argument. For example, they might take an ordinary sentence like 'All teenagers are lazy' and depict it as:

- All A are B

or:

- If P then Q

or:

- $(\forall x)(Tx \rightarrow Lx)$

Symbols like these can be a little scary to the newcomer to logic but by using such notation logicians can gain a greater degree of accuracy and objectivity in their analysis of an argument. They also use special techniques such as Venn diagrams and truth tables to test the validity of arguments. This requirement to fit ordinary sentences into formal symbolism, though, sometimes means that formal logic is limited in the scope of arguments that it can deal with.

Critical thinking on the other hand is all about the more informal method of studying statements and arguments in their natural habitat. It tends to concentrate on ordinary language arguments, as they might appear in books, newspapers or TV shows. It will also often base its assessment of an argument on a non-symbolic interpretation of it.

Both of these approaches are equally useful ways of approaching the study of arguments and this Book will draw on the most useful aspects of each approach. What formal logic gains in precision is arguably bought at the cost of straying too far from the richness and variety of natural languages. What critical thinking gains in capturing arguments as they appear in context, it loses in exactness and objectivity. This is why critical thinking is sometimes seen as being as much of an art as it is a science. The skill of interpreting an argument as it appears in everyday speech is one that involves a certain degree of practice to acquire. This practice will take the form of examining a number of examples and assessing how reliable they are.

Critical Thinking in Action

The best way to appreciate what critical thinking involves, and thereby understand how important it is, is to see it in operation with the use of some concrete examples. Let us examine a number of arguments taken from everyday life to see how a careful analysis of them can uncover common mistakes.

Example 1

- 'Everyone knows that the job of prime minister involves working long hours. Everyone also knows that children require their parent's full attention if they are to grow up to be emotionally stable adults. It surely follows then that women shouldn't really aim for high office if they want to have children.'

This argument is making an error but initially it may not be obvious what it is. The argument starts with some reasonable claims but then deduces an objectionable conclusion from these claims. What has gone wrong here is that the opening claim that 'children require their parent's full attention' is making a claim about parents in *general* but then goes on to use it to make a point about women in *particular*. If both of the opening claims are true then it is as effective an argument against fathers becoming prime minister, as it is against mothers. The argument therefore doesn't give us enough reasons to pick out women as being especially affected by the demands of high office.

Example 2

- 'Carl Jung is one of the foremost psychological theorists of the last 100 years yet we should approach his theories with extreme caution. Before the war he worked as an editor for a publication which supported the Nazi's by endorsing Hitler's autobiography *Mein Kampf*.'

This second argument draws a dubious link between the validity of Jung's psychology and his political associations. It is of course perfectly possible that Jung's views on psychology could nonetheless be valid regardless of whether he was a Nazi sympathiser or not[1]. This sort of mistake is known as **attacking the person**. This is when someone tries to win an argument by attacking the person they are arguing against rather than the point that the person supports.

---

[1] Jung later said that his publication had to endorse Hitler's autobiography *Mein Kampf* to ensure the survival of his profession during the Nazi era.

Example 3

- 'Have you every heard the saying, 'Sticks and stones will break by bones but names will never hurt me'? What it means is that words are essentially harmless. Racism, sexism and sectarianism are just words too, so they are all essentially harmless.'

This argument is guilty of a mistake known as **equivocation**. This is when an argument uses a word that has two distinct meanings. This becomes a problem when the reliability of the argument rests on a confusion of these two meanings. The problem word here is 'racism', which is really referring to two different things in this argument. First, there is 'racism the word', and second, there is 'racism the practise.' Racism the word is indeed harmless but racism the practise or activity is far from harmless. The practise of racism can lead to discrimination against minority groups; aggressive behaviour and even the murder of innocent people. The argument fails to distinguish clearly between these two uses of the term racism and so fails to reliably support its conclusion.

More examples of bad arguments will be examined in Chapter 6. However, having considered these few examples above, it should hopefully be apparent how a careful analysis of language can protect us from making mistakes. Moreover, it should also be plain how a lack of concern for clarity of expression can have a very real impact on our everyday lives.

Chapter Summary

✓ Critical thinking is the art of evaluating arguments.

✓ Evaluating arguments involves clarifying their structure and assessing how well they support their conclusions.

✓ Critical thinking first originated as an offshoot of philosophy.

✓ Critical thinking is useful in a number of modern day professions.

✓ Critical thinking is an informal approach to the study of logic.

Exercises

Answers to the following exercises can be found at the end of this chapter. If you have any difficulties with any of these questions refer back to the text of Chapter 1.

Exercise 1.1

Answer the following questions in your own words:

1.   What sorts of activity does critical thinking involve?

2.   Which academic subject is critical thinking a central component of?

3.   Why is it useful to study critical thinking?

4.   Which ancient Greek philosopher is often credited with the early development of critical thinking?

5.   What is a 'syllogism'?

6.   Give an example of a syllogism which you have invented yourself.

7.   What is the difference between critical thinking and logic?

8.   Why do logicians sometimes use special symbols to represent arguments?

9.   What is wrong with arguments that are guilty of 'attacking the person'?

10. What is meant by the term 'equivocation' in an argument?

Answers

Answers to Exercise 1.1

1. *Critical thinking includes: evaluating arguments; identifying the component parts of arguments; making hidden premises explicit; clarifying the structure of arguments; evaluating the validity and soundness of arguments; exposing fallacies.*

2. *Philosophy.*

3. *The study of critical thinking will make you a better philosopher and better at debate in other subjects too. It is also a good preparation for a number of careers such as law or journalism and it will make you better at assessing political arguments too.*

4. *Aristotle.*

5. *A syllogism is a type of three line argument popularised by Aristotle.*

6. *Any suitable example such as: 'All cats are choosy. Brixy is a cat, so Brixy is choosy.'*

7. *Critical thinking is an informal approach to the study of arguments whereas logic is a more formal study of arguments using technical notation and diagrams.*

8. *By using special symbols logicians can more accurately depict the form of arguments and so gain a greater degree of precision in their analysis of them.*

9. *Arguments which attack the person concentrate on undermining the character of their opponent rather than the particular claim that their opponents support.*

10. *Equivocation occurs when an argument uses a word or term which has a double meaning and the reliability of the argument depends upon them having the same meaning.*

Chapter 2

Statements and Arguments

What is a Statement?

A **statement** is a type of sentence. However, not all sentences are statements. In critical thinking we use the term statement to describe sentences that have a **truth-value**. In other words, statements are sentences capable of being **true** or **false**. It is not the case, though, that all sentences are capable of this. This is because sentences perform all sorts of different functions in the English language (and in other languages too). We can use words and sentences to state facts; to give vent to our feelings; to ask questions; to say prayers; to issue commands or to sing a song. For example:

- Stating facts: 'Cairo is the capital city of Egypt.'
- Giving vent to emotions: 'Yippee!'
- Asking questions: 'What sort of music do you like?'
- Issuing commands: 'Clean up your room!'

Experts in the study of language, known as linguists, divide all sentences into four broad groupings: **declarative** sentences (statements); **interrogative** sentences (questions); **imperative** sentences (commands); and **exclamatory** sentences (exclamations).

In the above list only the first one is a proper statement. A sentence can only be true or false if it is making a claim about the world so, 'Cairo is the capital city of Egypt', is making a claim about the world and this claim can either be true, if it *is* the capital city, or false if it *isn't*. Either way this sentence qualifies as being a statement. Thus, only declarative sentences can be statements. The rest of the above examples cannot be true or false because they aren't stating any facts. They instead have a different function altogether. The purpose of a command, for example, is to provoke some form of behaviour or to get someone to do something. To say 'False' in response to the command 'Clean up your room' would be to misunderstand the function of commands. Similarly, the purpose of a question is to discover some piece of information, so to say 'False' in response to the question 'What sort of music do you like?' would be to misunderstand the function of questions.

In logic the term **proposition** is also often used in preference to the term statement.

This is because some logicians wish to highlight the fact that many different sentences or statements can express the same underlying claim or proposition. For example, consider the following sentences:

- 'I like pop music.'
- 'Pop music is my favourite.'
- 'J'adore le pop music.'

All of these sentences mean the same thing and so they are all expressing the same proposition. They are just using different words or grammatical structures to do so. This difference in mode of expression, though, won't make any difference to the arguments in which they appear: they are all performing the same job and will all have the same truth-value. For our purposes, then, the terms 'statement' and 'proposition' will be used interchangeably to mean a 'sentence with a truth-value' or a 'declarative sentence.'

The Importance of Statements

It is important to be clear what statements are because arguments can only be composed of statements. Arguments cannot be composed entirely of commands and questions: if they were they wouldn't be saying anything about the world. Of course, in real life people *do* occasionally insert questions or commands in the middle of an argument, but on these occasions they usually contribute nothing to the argument itself and their argument would work just as effectively without them. Consider the following example:

- 'I think torture is wrong. If we allow torture then innocent people will be tortured. Would you like to be tortured? Stop torture now!'

This argument actually only contains two statements: 'I think torture is wrong' and 'if we allow torture then innocent people will be tortured.' Taken together, these statements function perfectly well as an argument. The question 'Would you like to be tortured?' and the command 'Stop torture now!' don't really contribute anything else.

At best, we might say that the question 'Would you like to be tortured' is a **rhetorical question** and these have a slightly different function from ordinary questions. Rhetorical questions aren't really meant to be answered because their answer so obvious (clearly we *wouldn't* like to be tortured) so they could be regarded as a covert way of expressing a particular statement. So, the question 'Would you like to be tortured?' might be read as shorthand for the statement 'You *wouldn't* like to be tortured', which could contribute another reason for disagreeing with the use of torture and so play a useful role in this argument. However, notice that the only way that a question has been useful in an argument is *after* we have converted it into a statement. This supports our original contention that only statements can create arguments.

What is an Argument?

An argument is a collection of statements that are put forward in support of some further statement. For example:

- All crocodiles are reptiles
  All reptiles are vertebrates[2]
  Thus, all crocodiles are vertebrates

Arguments have the potential of getting others to agree to something that they initially rejected, using statements that they do agree with. Someone who agreed that all crocodiles were reptiles and that all reptiles were vertebrates might not initially agree that all crocodiles were vertebrates, until an argument was constructed that made it clear that the first two beliefs imply the third.

The Difference between Statements and Arguments

Arguments are more powerful tools than individual statements. The purpose of an argument is to **establish** a point rather than just **asserting** that something is true. There is a big difference between simply stating, 'All crocodiles are vertebrates' and arguing 'all crocodiles are reptiles and all reptiles are vertebrates, hence all crocodiles are vertebrates.' Arguments provide support or give reasons for the claims that they make.

Consider the following exchange:

- *Rachel*: 'Your team will lose today.'
  Antoinette: 'No they won't.'
  Rachel: 'Yes they will!'
  Antoinette: 'No they won't!'

---

[2] Vertebrates are any creature with a backbone or spine.

This is what many people often think of when you talk about 'arguments' because, in the 'disagreement' sense of the word argument, Rachel is 'arguing' with Antoinette. However, strictly speaking, neither Rachel nor Antoinette provides any real arguments at all. Rachel is merely asserting that one statement is true while Antoinette is simply denying it.

Now consider this next exchange:

- *Rachel*: 'Your team will lose today.'
  Antoinette: 'No they won't.'
  Rachel: 'Yes they will. You're missing all your best players and you can't win without them.'
  Antoinette: 'No they won't. Our substitute players are just as good and have never lost a game.'

This time Rachel has backed up her bald assertion with *reasons* and is therefore attempting to *prove* that her initial claim is true. Antoinette is also attempting to *refute* it with reasons of her own.

At best, then, individual statements can only **assert** or **deny** that something is the case. Arguments, on the other hand, can be said to either **prove** or **refute** that something is the case, because they have backed up their assertions with reasons. To simply assert that something is false isn't the same thing as proving that something is false.

Premises and Conclusions

The statements in an argument can be categorised as either **premises** or **conclusions**. The conclusion is the central claim that the argument is designed to establish. The premises are the reasons given in support of this conclusion. In the crocodile argument the premises are the statements 'All crocodiles are reptiles' and 'All reptiles are vertebrates.' The conclusion is the statement 'All crocodiles are vertebrates':

- All crocodiles are reptiles – *Premise*
  All reptiles are vertebrates – *Premise*
  Thus, all crocodiles are vertebrates – *Conclusion*

In this particular argument there are two premises and one conclusion. However, it is possible for arguments to have any number of premises depending on how sophisticated the argument is. In theory, arguments could have one premise or a million premises. Moreover, complex arguments could have more than one conclusion or they could make use of sub-conclusions, which they might establish in order to prove some further conclusion.

Ordinary Language Arguments

In critical thinking, we often use examples, like the crocodile argument above, where the premises and the conclusion are neatly laid out in sequential order with the premises at the start and conclusion at the end. However, in real life our use of language is much more messy that this. In ordinary language we might provide the conclusion at the outset and then provide the reasons later, or we might bury the conclusion in the middle of the argument. Consider the following example:

- 'I failed my driving test. Now you think I'm stupid. You always said that anyone who fails their driving test is stupid.'

This argument is a bit more realistic and doesn't look like something you might find in logic textbooks. In this argument the speaker has started with a premise, then given us his conclusion, and then provided further support for the conclusion with a second premise. However, we could tidy it up to make it easier to see what is going on:

- I failed my driving test – *premise*
  You think anyone who fails their driving test is stupid – *premise*
  Therefore, you think I am stupid – *conclusion*

This process of 'tidying up' **ordinary language arguments** requires a certain degree of interpretation on the part of the critical thinker. This is why critical thinking is an art that requires skill to see past ordinary modes of expression and grasp the essential points that an argument is making.

Identifying Premises and Conclusions

How do we know which lines of an argument are premises and which are conclusions in an ordinary language argument? Sometimes we can't tell and we just have to make a judgement based on the context in which the statements appear. However, most premises and conclusions have **indicator words** that provide a hint as to whether the statement is functioning as a premise or as a conclusion.

Because *premises* are statements that give a reason in support of a conclusion, they usually begin with words or phrases like:

- The reason is…
- Given that…
- In view of the fact that…
- Because…
- Since…
- As…

Conclusions on the other hand are attempting to infer some claim from the preceding premises so often begin with words or phrases like:

- Therefore…
- Thus…
- So…
- Consequently…
- Hence…
- Accordingly…

Of course, there are no particular indicator words that premises or conclusions *have* to possess, and indeed some premises and conclusions will have no indicator words at all. In such cases we must resort to looking at the context in which the statement appears in order to ascertain whether it is a premise or a conclusion. If this offers no clues then we have no remaining options other than asking the author of the argument the function they intended each statement to perform.

Hidden or Suppressed Premises

Another feature of ordinary language arguments is that in everyday speech we don't always make our premises explicit. Sometimes premises are so obvious that they don't need to be stated at all. However, one skill we must acquire in order to become good at critical thinking is the ability to identify any unstated premises that an argument might be relying on to be considered technically valid. These premises are called hidden or suppressed or assumed premises. For example:

- 'I think dogs are dangerous, so they should be kept away from young children.'

In this argument the premise is 'I think dogs are dangerous' and the conclusion is 'They should be kept away from young children.' However, the argument really relies on a hidden premise for its validity, which is perhaps so obvious that the speaker felt that they needn't spell it out. The hidden premise is 'Dangerous things should be kept away from children.' Once we supply this hidden or assumed premise we can tidy up the argument as shown below. The hidden premise is in brackets:

- Dogs are dangerous
  (Dangerous things should be kept away from children)
  Therefore, dogs should be kept away from children

Chapter Summary

✓ A statement is a sentence with a truth-value (i.e. it can be true or false).

✓ Questions, commands and exclamations do not have a truth-value.

✓ Only statements can therefore make a contribution to an argument.

✓ Rhetorical questions can be a covert way of expressing a statement.

✓ An argument is a collection of statements.

✓ The premises of an argument are the reasons given in support of the conclusion.

✓ The conclusion of an argument is the central claim that the argument is designed to support.

✓ A statement can only assert or deny something but an argument can prove or refute something.

✓ Ordinary language arguments do not always present their premises in a conventional way.

✓ Indicator words can be used to identify which lines of an argument are premises and which are conclusions.

✓ A hidden premise is an assumed claim that the argument relies upon for its validity but is not explicitly stated.

Exercises

Answers to the following exercises can be found at the end of this chapter. If you have any difficulties with any of these questions refer back to the text of Chapter 2.

Exercise 2.1

Answer the following questions in your own words:

1. What is the difference between a sentence and a statement?

2. Give an example of a sentence that is not a statement.

3. What is a 'rhetorical' question?

4. What is an argument?

5. What is the difference between 'asserting' a point and 'proving' a point?

6. How do 'ordinary language arguments' vary from textbook examples?

7. Provide two indicator words that might identify a statement as a premise.

8. Provide two indicator words that might identify a statement as a conclusion.

9. What is a 'hidden' or 'assumed' premise?

10. Invent an argument of your own that relies on a hidden premise. State clearly what the hidden premise is.

Exercise 2.2

A statement is a sentence that is capable of being true or false. Identify which of the following sentences are statements and which are not:

1. Most cats have tails.

2. $3 \times 7 = 21$.

3. How do you feel this morning?

4. All Scotsmen wear kilts.

5. Leave, now!

6. Julius Caesar died in 55 BC.

7. I love you!

8. Berlin is the capital of Germany.

9.   I could do with a rest!

10. Ghosts exist.

Exercise 2.3

An argument is a conclusion supported by reasons. Which of the following are arguments and which are not?

1.   I can't stand milkshakes because they make me sick.

2.   She doesn't have insurance, she never crosses when there is a green man and she never wears a seatbelt. I think Jennifer is a very reckless person.

3.   You must be the greediest person I have ever met.

4.   This shape is a triangle because its angles add up to 180 degrees.

5.   Most people in Britain couldn't tell you whether the Labour Party is for or against Europe.

6.   The cat lay on the kitchen floor. It purred contentedly.

7.   Get up, get your coat and get in the car.

8.   How can you say you don't love me? How can you tell me that kiss meant nothing? How can you go out with someone else?

9.   I'm not going on holiday. I'm broke.

10. If you smoke cigarettes you will damage your health.

Exercise 2.4

Identify the premises and conclusions in the following arguments:

1.   All dogs are mammals. Fido is a dog. Therefore, Fido is a mammal.

2.   Oranges are good for you. The reason being that all citrus fruit is good for you and oranges are a citrus fruit.

3.   The last 3 goldfish I owned all died. So, don't buy me any more goldfish since I am clearly the world's worst goldfish owner.

4.   Imran must be Scottish. He is a British citizen and he isn't English, Welsh or Northern Irish.

5.   If you don't pass your exams you won't get into university and if you don't get to university you won't get a degree. So, you need to pass your exams.

6. The Loch Ness monster doesn't exist since no one has ever caught it and most sightings are from unreliable witnesses.

7. James renewed his passport. He also bought a ticket to New York and he packed his bags. Consequently, I think James is planning to leave the country.

8. This tree is an oak because all oaks produce acorns and this tree has acorns.

9. Since I burnt the toast you think I'm hopeless. After all, you think anyone who can't cook is hopeless.

10. Van Gogh is the greatest painter to have lived. Why? His paintings fetch the most at auction. He is revered throughout the world. Posters of his images adorn millions of homes. Hence, I think Van Gogh is the greatest painter to have lived.

Exercise 2.5

The following arguments all rely on hidden or suppressed premises. Suggest in each case what the hidden premise might be.

1. Fido is a dog so he must be carnivorous.

2. You are a smoker so you are not likely to live long.

3. I don't drink alcohol because I am on antibiotics.

4. You shouldn't touch him. He's contagious.

5. Of course the flowers died! You watered them with petrol!

6. Well done! You drank all your milk. You'll grow up to have strong bones now.

7. The power station should be closed because it pollutes the environment.

8. You should always put rubbish away properly because we don't want to attract rats.

9. You shouldn't stand out in the rain. You'll catch a cold.

10. Don't vote SNP unless you want to pay more tax.

Answers

Answers to Exercise 2.1

1. *A statement is a sentence that is capable of having a truth value, whereas a sentence is any coherent utterance which could include ones that do not have a truth value.*

2. *Any suitable examples. Exclamations such as 'Hooray for Jack!', questions such as 'Do you like Sean Connery?', and commands such as 'sit down' all lack a truth value.*

3. *A rhetorical question is one that is not intended to be answered as the answer is deemed to be obvious.*

4. *An argument is a collection of statements or propositions. Some of these statements are premises, which are reasons given in support of the conclusion, the central claim of the argument.*

5. *To assert a point is to simply make a claim without giving any support for it. To prove a point is to back up your claim with reasons.*

6. *Ordinary language arguments are generally more realistic than many textbook examples. They may not be articulated clearly, they may not provide the premises and conclusions in a conventional order and they may make use of hidden premises.*

7. *Any two suitable examples such as: 'since', 'because', 'as', etc.*

8. *Any two suitable examples such as: 'thus', 'therefore', 'hence', etc.*

9. *A hidden premise is one that an argument relies on but is not explicitly stated by the arguer. Usually hidden premises are so obvious they do not need spelling out.*

10. *Any suitable example such as: 'The factory should be shut down because it is polluting the river', which makes use of the hidden premise 'Anything which pollutes the river should be shut down.'*

Answers to Exercise 2.2

1. *Most cats have tails – a statement.*

2. *3 x 7 = 21 – a statement.*

3. *How do you feel this morning? – not a statement, a question.*

4. *All Scotsmen wear kilts – a statement.*

5. *Leave, now! – not a statement, a command.*

6. *Julius Caesar died in 55 BC – a statement.*

7. *I love you! – a statement (either it is true that I love you or it is false).*

8. *Berlin is the capital of Germany – a statement.*

9. *I could do with a rest! – a statement (either it is true that I could do with a rest or it isn't).*

10. *Ghosts exist – a statement (either it is true that ghosts exist or it isn't).*

Answers to Exercise 2.3

1. *I can't stand milkshakes because they make me sick – an argument.*

2. *She doesn't have insurance, she never crosses when there is a green man and she never wears a seatbelt. I think Jennifer is a very reckless person – an argument.*

3. *You must be the greediest person I have ever met – not an argument, just a statement.*

4. *This shape is a triangle because its angles add up to 180 degrees – an argument.*

5. *Most people in Britain couldn't tell you whether the Labour Party is for or against Europe – not an argument, just a statement.*

6. *The cat lay on the kitchen floor. It purred contentedly – not an argument, just a pair of statements.*

7. *Get up, get your coat and get in the car – not an argument, just a series of commands.*

8. *How can you say you don't love me? How can you tell me that kiss meant nothing? How can you go out with someone else? – not an argument, just a series of questions.*

9. *I'm not going on holiday. I'm broke – an argument.*

10. *If you smoke cigarettes you will damage your health – not an argument, just a statement.*

Answers to Exercise 2.4

1. Premises: 'All dogs are mammals' and 'Fido is a dog.'
    Conclusion: 'Therefore, Fido is a mammal.'

2. Premises: 'The reason being that all citrus fruit is good for you' and 'oranges are a citrus fruit.'
    Conclusion: 'Oranges are good for you.'

3. Premises: 'The last 3 goldfish I owned all died' and 'since I am clearly the world's worst goldfish owner.'
    Conclusion: 'So, don't buy me any more goldfish.'

4. Premises: 'He is a British citizen' and 'he isn't English, Welsh or Northern Irish.' Conclusion: 'Imran must be Scottish.'

5. Premises: 'If you don't pass your exams you won't get into university' and 'if you don't get to university you won't get a degree.'
    Conclusion: 'So, you need to pass your exams.'

6. Premises: 'since no one has ever caught it' and 'most sightings are from unreliable witnesses.'
    Conclusion: 'The Loch Ness monster doesn't exist.'

7. Premises: 'James renewed his passport' and 'He also bought a ticket to New York' and 'he packed his bags.'
    Conclusion: 'Consequently, I think James is planning to leave the country.'

8. Premises: 'because all oaks produce acorns' and 'this tree has acorns.'
    Conclusion: 'This tree is an oak.'

9. Premises: 'Since I burnt the toast' and 'After all, you think anyone who can't cook is hopeless.'
    Conclusion: 'you think I'm hopeless.'

10. Premises: 'His paintings fetch the most at auction' and 'He is revered throughout the world' and 'Posters of his images adorn millions of homes.'
    Conclusion: 'Hence, I think Van Gogh is the greatest painter to have lived' and 'Van Gogh is the greatest painter to have lived.' Notice how this argument states the conclusion twice, once at the outset and again at the end.

Answers to Exercise 2.5

1. *All dogs are carnivorous.*

2. *Smoking shortens life expectancy.*

3. *People on antibiotics shouldn't drink alcohol.*

4. *If you touch a contagious person you will be infected.*

5. *If you water flowers with petrol they will die.*

6. *Drinking milk helps strengthen bones.*

7. *Things which pollute the environment should be closed down.*

8. *Rubbish attracts rats.*

9. *Standing out in the rain can cause you to catch a cold.*

10. *The SNP want to increase tax.*

Chapter 3

Reliable and Unreliable Arguments

What Makes a Reliable Argument?

An argument can be reliable in a number of different ways. Good arguments are persuasive and if well designed can force others to accept the point you are trying to make. However, in critical thinking we need to be more precise about what we mean when we say an argument is 'reliable'. There are two major virtues that an argument can have: the argument can be *well structured* and the argument can contain *true statements*.

If an argument is well structured it is called a **valid argument**. Badly structured arguments are known as **invalid arguments**. However, it is possible for an argument to be well structured without being convincing. This might happen if the argument contains false premises. We therefore call an argument with both a valid structure and true premises a **sound argument** and these are the most reliable arguments of all. If an argument has either false premises or an invalid structure it is described as being **unsound**. These concepts require a fuller explanation, however.

Validity

An argument is valid if it is well structured, but what do we mean by the term 'well structured'? A well-structured argument is one that forces you to accept its conclusion if you accept its premises. In a valid argument, the premises *compel* you to agree with the conclusion on pain of contradiction (so long as you accept the premises). Consider the following valid argument:

- All monkeys are mammals
  Charlie is a monkey
  Therefore, Charlie is a mammal

If we accept the opening premise, 'All monkeys are mammals', and we agree, 'Charlie is a monkey', then we must accept 'Charlie is a mammal' or we would be guilty of contradicting ourselves. The only way to reject the conclusion would be to deny one of the two premises. In a valid argument, accepting the premises locks us in to the conclusion because the conclusion is in fact embedded in the premises.

One way of describing the relationship between premises and conclusions in a valid argument is to say that in a valid argument the conclusion has been correctly **inferred** from the premises or that the conclusion has been properly **drawn** from the premises.

Most students of critical thinking get confused about validity because they think it means that the argument must have a true conclusion. However, validity is only a measure of how well structured an argument is, not whether its individual lines are true or not. We only said that *if* you accept the premises of a valid argument *then* you will be committed to its conclusion. This is not to say, however, that an argument couldn't still be well structured even if it had false premises. Consider the following example:

- All Frenchmen speak Chinese
  Brad Pitt is French
  Therefore, Brad Pitt speaks Chinese

This is also a valid argument despite the fact that every line of the argument is false. The falsity of the individual statements in the argument does not prevent it from being well structured. The premises still lock us into the conclusion in the same way as they did in the monkey argument. If it *had been* the case that all Frenchmen spoke Chinese, and that Brad Pitt was a Frenchman, then it *would have been* the case that Brad Pitt spoke Chinese: the fact that he isn't and he can't does not stop it being a valid argument. In fact, you could disagree with everything that someone said but still agree that all their arguments were valid.

Invalidity

An argument is invalid if it is badly structured. A badly structured argument is one where the premises *do not* tie you in to the conclusion. In an invalid argument we are not forced to accept the conclusion, even on occasions where we have accepted that all the premises are true. Consider the following example carefully (compare it with the previous monkey argument if you wish):

- All monkeys are mammals
  Charlie is a mammal
  Therefore, Charlie is a monkey

This argument is invalid because even though all monkeys are mammals, it does not follow that all mammals must therefore be monkeys. So, the fact that Charlie is a mammal is not enough to *guarantee* that Charlie is a monkey. Even if we accept the premises, we would not be contradicting ourselves if we insisted on denying the conclusion. Valid arguments must do more than make the conclusion a *possible* consequence of the premises: they must make the conclusion a *necessary* consequence.

Just as we mustn't confuse validity with truth, we should never confuse invalidity with falsity. Remember, validity is simply a description of how well structured an argument is, not whether its component statements are true or false. This means that it is possible to have an argument where every statement is true, yet the argument remains invalid. Consider the following example:

- All Frenchmen are French
  All Scotsmen are Scottish
  Therefore, all monkeys are mammals

This argument is clearly invalid even though every statement within the argument is true. Although it is true that all monkeys are mammals, it is not true in virtue of those particular premises. The premises in this argument do nothing to guarantee the truth of the conclusion, hence the argument is invalid.

The above argument appears to be obviously invalid, but consider the following example:

- All humans have bones
  All Scotsmen have bones
  Therefore, all Scotsmen are human

This example is also invalid although each statement is true. However, it is not obvious that the premises are entirely irrelevant to the conclusion. However, once we consider the structure of reasoning in this argument it becomes clear that even though all humans do have bones, the presence of bones in Scotsmen is not what makes them human. After all, hamsters, chickens and kangaroos all have bones, but this does not make them human. The opening premises would have had to say '*Only* humans have bones' before the presence of bones in Scotsmen would be enough to render them human.

Validity and Truth

In critical thinking we must never confuse validity with truth. Only arguments can be valid or invalid and only statements can be true or false. Strictly speaking, there is no such thing as a 'valid statement' and there is no such thing as a 'true argument'.

A statement is true when it accurately describes some state of affairs and false when it doesn't[3]. Validity on the other hand is a measure of the structure of the argument. Arguments can't be described as 'true' because arguments are composed of lots of statements, some of which might be true and some of which might be false. This might seem a little odd at first since in everyday speech you might have heard people say things like 'Jane's argument is very true' or that 'Farheen made a valid point.' However, in critical thinking we must be less sloppy in our use of language and restrict our use of the words 'valid' and 'invalid' to describing the structure of arguments, and the words 'true' or 'false' to describing the accuracy of statements.

However, whilst it is correct to say that validity and truth are not the same things, there is an *indirect* relationship between validity and truth that is only apparent when we examine valid arguments. In an invalid argument there is no relationship between the truth or falsity of the premises and the invalidity of the structure. Because invalid arguments are badly structured, it is possible to have any combination of truth and falsity between the premises and the conclusion in an invalid argument: you could have false premises with a false conclusion; true premises with a true conclusion; true premises with a false conclusion or false premises with a true conclusion.

In valid arguments, though, there is one truth combination that is impossible: valid arguments *cannot* have true premises followed by a false conclusion. If an argument is well structured, true premises should *guarantee* a true conclusion, so the minute we see an argument with true premises and a false conclusion we can automatically say that the argument must, by definition, be invalid. This asymmetrical relationship between validity and truth is summarised below. Every combination is possible in valid arguments except number 4.

1. Valid structure + True premises + True conclusion ✔
2. Valid structure + False premises + False conclusion ✔
3. Valid structure + True premises + False conclusion ✔
4. Valid structure + False premises + True conclusion ✘
5. Invalid structure + True premises + True conclusion ✔
6. Invalid structure + False premises + False conclusion ✔
7. Invalid structure + True premises + False conclusion ✔
8. Invalid structure + False premises + True conclusion ✔

---

[3] Those who have previously studied philosophy may be aware that there are in fact a number of rival definitions of truth (e.g. the coherentist theory; the pragmatist theory; the correspondence theory). However, this discussion is out with the scope of this text and for our purposes it will suffice to assume that a statement is true when it matches the world and false when it doesn't.

Soundness

An argument is said to be sound if its premises are true and it has a valid structure. A **sound argument** is therefore the best sort of argument you can have. Since sound arguments have both a valid structure and true premises we are also guaranteed that they will have true conclusions too. Consider the following examples:

- All cats are lizards
  All lizards are birds
  Therefore, all cats are birds

- All cats are mammals
  All mammals are vertebrates
  Therefore, all cats are vertebrates

The first argument, while valid, is not sound. It is not sound because both the premises are false (cats are not lizards and lizards are not birds). The conclusion has been correctly inferred from the premises, but we cannot necessarily depend on it because it is based on false claims. The second argument, however, has both a valid structure and true premises. We can therefore place more faith in the conclusion, as the argument is sound.

Unsound Arguments

Because sound arguments require two ingredients to qualify as being sound, there is therefore more than one way for an argument to be rendered unsound. An argument is unsound if it either has false premises or an invalid form, or both. Consider the following examples:

1. All parrots are cats
   All cats have feathers
   Therefore, all parrots have feathers

2. All parrots are birds
   All parrots have feathers
   Therefore, all birds have feathers

3. All parrots are cats
   All parrots have feathers
   Therefore, all cats have feathers

All these arguments are unsound, but each for a different reason. The first is valid but its premises are false. The second has true premises and a true conclusion but has an invalid structure. The third has both false premises and an invalid structure.

Deciding whether an argument is sound or unsound isn't always easy. If you are good at critical thinking you might be able to determine if an argument is valid but you will need some factual knowledge to say whether it is sound or not. For example, you will need a good knowledge of History to say whether the premise 'Mary Queen of Scots was executed in 1587' is true or not, and this would have to be established before you could then go on to determine whether any arguments that this statement appears in are sound or not. Notice, however, that once you determine that an argument is invalid, the issue of assessing the truth of the premises doesn't arise. All invalid arguments are unsound while only some valid arguments are unsound.

Deductive and Inductive Arguments

Some arguments are said to be **deductive** in nature and others are said to be **inductive**. Induction and deduction are two different sorts of reasoning. Most of the arguments we have been looking at so far have been examples of *de*ductive reasoning. However, a large number of arguments that we use in real life are *in*ductive in nature. Inductive arguments are arguments based on experience. Without using induction as well as deduction, many of the conclusions of science would be impossible. Let us examine a few examples:

Deduction: All cats have tails
               Felix is a cat
               Therefore, Felix has a tail

Induction: Felix has a tail
               Felix is a cat
               Therefore, all cats have tails

Deductive arguments usually begin with a very general premise and then go on to deduce the truth of some particular fact based on this general claim. Notice how the first argument above starts by talking about *all* cats and then uses this to draw conclusions about a *particular* cat, Felix. Inductive arguments on the other hand usually work the other way around. They begin with some particular premise, which is based on a limited number of experiences and then use this as the basis of some universal claim about the world. In the example above, the argument begins with some *particular* observations of Felix and then goes on to infer general conclusions about *all* cats based on these limited observations.

Deductive Arguments

In deductive arguments the conclusion does not go beyond what is contained in the premises. If we assume the truth of the original premise, and the argument is properly structured, then we are compelled to accept the conclusion in a valid deductive argument. This means that the conclusion of a deductive argument is capable of being **certain**. The most common defining features of valid deductive arguments are as follows:

- They use universal premises to prove particular conclusions.
- Their conclusion doesn't claim more than their premises.
- They cannot yield a false conclusion when the premises are true.
- They are therefore capable of being described as valid arguments.
- Their conclusions are capable of being certain truths.

Inductive Arguments

Inductive arguments, though, are less reliable. Even if the premises of the inductive argument are true, we are still not guaranteed that the conclusion of the argument is true. In fact, even if an inductive argument was based on the observation of a million cats, we could still not be certain that any conclusions we inferred about cats would be certain. This is because of a difficulty known as the **problem of induction**.

The problem of induction arises because the number of observations we can have is always finite. Say I observe a million cats and they all turn out to have tails. Am I justified in concluding that all cats have tails? The answer is that I am not because it is always a possibility that the next cat I observe (the $1,000,001^{st}$ cat) might not have a tail. This means that the conclusions of inductive arguments can never be certain, only **probable**. Obviously, conclusions based on a million cats are more probable than conclusions based on the observation one cat, but no matter how high the probability gets it will never reach the point where I can be *guaranteed* that my conclusions are certain.

This weakness of inductive arguments has a number of consequences for our treatment of critical thinking. If we are never guaranteed true conclusions in an inductive argument then, strictly speaking, this means that inductive arguments can never be valid, according to our definition of validity. Worse still, if inductive arguments can never be valid, then this also means that they can never be sound either, given our definition of soundness.

Of course, this is not to say that inductive arguments are therefore useless. For example, consider the argument below drawn from the world of medicine:

- 'Every schizophrenic patient treated with clozapine has reported a reduction in symptoms. Therefore, clozapine is an effective treatment for schizophrenia.'

In fact in all the natural sciences (such as Biology, Chemistry, Physics) and in all the social sciences (such as Psychology, Sociology and Economics) we use inductive arguments all the time because they are in fact fruitful ways of discovering all sorts of facts about ourselves and the world. The fact that they are based on inductive reasoning, though, means that we must be willing to revise them in light of any future contradictory observations.

The most common defining features of inductive arguments are as follows:

- They use particular premises to prove universal conclusions.
- Their conclusion goes beyond what is contained in their premises.
- They can yield a false conclusion even when their premises are true.
- They are therefore all technically invalid arguments.
- They are also therefore all technically unsound arguments.
- Their conclusions can only ever be probable, not certain.

One response to the unsettling consequence that many scientific arguments are invalid and unsound is to use a different set of criteria when evaluating inductive arguments. This is why some logicians prefer using the terms **reliable** and **unreliable** rather than valid and invalid when discussing such arguments. They also suggest assessing inductive arguments in terms of their **strength** or **weakness** rather than their soundness. This recognises the fact that while inductive arguments might not be valid they can still be very reliable and they are still worth investigating to assess how strong or weak their conclusions are. This approach has led to the development of whole new branches of logic dedicated to the study of inductive rather than deductive arguments.

Chapter Summary

✓   A valid argument is well structured and guarantees a true conclusion provided the premises are true.

✓   An invalid argument is one that is badly structured and does not guarantee a true conclusion, even when all the premises are true.

✓   Only whole arguments can be valid or invalid, they cannot be true or false.

✓   Only individual statements can be true or false, they cannot be valid or invalid.

✓   A sound argument has a valid structure and true premises.

✓   An unsound argument has either an invalid structure, or a false premise or both.

✓   Arguments can be classified as either inductive or deductive in nature.

✓   A deductive argument attempts to derive its conclusion from what is contained in the premises alone.

✓   An inductive argument attempts to go beyond its premises by generalising from a limited number of experiences.

Exercises

Answers to the following exercises can be found at the end of this chapter. If you have any difficulties with any of these questions refer back to the text of Chapter 3.

Exercise 3.1

Answer the following questions in your own words:

1. What is a valid argument?
2. What is an invalid argument?
3. What is the difference between a valid argument and a sound argument?
4. What two things could render an argument unsound?
5. How is it possible for a valid argument to have a false conclusion?
6. What is a deductive argument?
7. Provide your own example of a deductive argument.
8. What is an inductive argument?
9. Provide your own example of an inductive argument.
10. Can inductive arguments be valid? Explain your answer.

Exercise 3.2

A valid argument is one which guarantees a true conclusion if the premises are true. State whether you think the following arguments are valid or invalid. Try to give a reason to support your answer.

1. All politicians are liars
   John is a politician
   Therefore, John is a liar

2. All cats are carnivorous
   Pickles is carnivorous
   So, Pickles must be a cat

3. All journalists are inquisitive
    You aren't a journalist
    So, you can't be inquisitive

4. All fish have gills
    Dolphins don't have gills
    So, they can't be fish

5. All mammals have ears
    All cats have ears
    So, all cats are mammals

6. If you like Charles Dickens then you'll love *A Tale of Two Cities*
    You hated *A Tale of Two Cities*
    So, you can't like Charles Dickens

7. If you are Scottish then you'll speak fluent Russian
    You are Scottish
    So, you will speak fluent Russian

8. If you are Welsh then you are sure to like rugby
    If you like rugby then you must like flower arranging
    So, if you are Welsh then you must like flower arranging

9. Some women are clever
    Some women are deceitful
    So, at least one woman is both clever and deceitful

10. Most men are honest
    Most men are stupid
    So, at least one man is both honest and stupid

Exercise 3.3

A sound argument is one which is both valid and has true premises. State whether you think the following arguments are sound or unsound. Try to give a reason to support your answer.

1. All poodles are dogs
    All dogs are mammals
    So, all poodles are mammals

2. All ballet dancers are female
    Darcey Bussell is a ballet dancer
    Therefore, Darcey Bussell is female

3. All French people are European
    Gordon Brown is European
    So, Gordon Brown must be French

4. All journalists are bakers
    All bakers are scuba divers
    So, all journalists are scuba divers

5. All fish have gills
    Dolphins aren't fish
    So, dolphins don't have gills

6. If you don't eat meat then you are a vegetarian
    If you are a vegetarian then you are not a carnivore
    So, if you don't eat meat then you are not a carnivore

7. If you are Scottish then you'll speak fluent Russian
    Sean Connery is Scottish
    So, Sean Connery will speak fluent Russian

8. If you are a goalkeeper then you are a footballer
    The Queen is not a footballer
    So, the Queen is not a goalkeeper

9. Some actors are rich
    Most actors are talented
    So, at least one actor is both rich and talented

10. Most cats have tails
    Most cats have ears
    Therefore, at least one cat has both ears and a tail

Exercise 3.4

State whether the following arguments are inductive or deductive. Try to give a reason to support your answer.

1. All men are mortal. Therefore, Socrates is mortal since he is a man.
2. Partick Thistle are an abysmal team so Scottish football can't be that great.
3. These pills worked the last time I tried them so they should do the trick.
4. Hillary Clinton must be an intelligent woman because she's a lawyer and all lawyers are clever people.
5. My cat just hates getting wet so I wouldn't give your cat a bath if I were you.
6. Every time I've eaten oysters I've been sick so oysters must always cause sickness.
7. All dogs are descended from wolves so Fido must be descended from wolves.
8. Water boils at 100 degrees in Edinburgh so it must boil at 100 degrees in Manchester.
9. Children play games to pass the time in modern day Rome, so the children of ancient Rome must have played games too.
10. All citrus fruits are tasty so kumquats must taste good since they are citrus fruits too.

Exercise 3.5

State whether the following claims are true or false:

1. An invalid argument can have true premises.
2. An invalid argument can have a true conclusion.
3. An invalid argument can be sound.
4. A valid argument can have true premises.
5. A valid argument can have a false conclusion.
6. A valid argument can have true premises and a false conclusion.
7. A sound argument can have a false conclusion.
8. A sound argument can have a false premise.
9. An unsound argument can have true premises and a true conclusion.
10. An unsound argument can be valid.

Answers

Answers to Exercise 3.1

1. A valid argument is one which is well structured and will guarantee a true conclusion if the premises are true.

2. An invalid argument is one which is badly structured and will not always guarantee a true conclusion even when all of the premises are true.

3. A valid argument is simply well structured but a sound argument has both a valid structure and true premises.

4. It could either be invalid or have at least one false premise.

5. A valid argument can have a false conclusion because validity is only a description of how well structured an argument is, not a description of whether its component statements are true. Thus, an argument could still be well structured even if every line is false. For example: 'All pigs are monkeys. All monkeys are green. Therefore, all pigs are green.'

6. A deductive argument is one which deduces a particular conclusion from an assumed premise. Valid deductive arguments do not claim more than is contained in the premises.

7. Any suitable example such as: 'All pigs are pink. Porky is a pig. Therefore, Porky is pink.'

8. An inductive argument is one that is based on experience. Inductive arguments usually go beyond what is claimed in the premises.

9. Any suitable example such as: 'Porky is pink. Porky is a pig. Therefore, all pigs are pink.'

10. Technically, inductive arguments can never be valid because it is always possible for true premises to yield a false conclusion in an inductive argument. For example, if all the pigs I have seen have been pink, it is still always possible that there are pigs I have not met yet that are some other colour. This difficulty is known as the problem of induction. Inductive arguments are therefore often described as being strong or weak rather than valid or invalid.

Answers to Exercise 3.2

1. Valid. If the premises are true the conclusion must be true. If every politician is a liar then John must be too as he's a politician.

2. Invalid. Although all cats are carnivorous, not all carnivores are cats. So, we can't assume that Pickles is a cat just because he is carnivorous.

3. *Invalid. The opening premise doesn't claim that journalists are the only people who can be inquisitive. So, the fact that you aren't a journalist doesn't prevent you from being inquisitive.*

4. *Valid. If every fish has gills then anything without gills can't be a fish.*

5. *Invalid. Although all mammals have ears it is still possible to have ears without being a mammal.*

6. *Valid. If everyone who loves Charles Dickens loves this book then anyone who hates the book must dislike Charles Dickens. Of course, in real life it is possible to like an author even when you dislike one of their books, but this would only have a bearing on the soundness of the argument, not its validity.*

7. *Valid. Even though the opening premise and the conclusion are likely to be false, the argument is still well structured. If the premises were true the conclusion would have to be true too.*

8. *Valid. If the premises were true, the conclusion would have to be true.*

9. *Invalid. The word 'some' is ambiguous and can mean one woman or a million women. We are therefore not guaranteed a true conclusion because we are not assured that the 'some women' in premise one share any members with the 'some women' in premise two.*

10. *Valid. The word 'most', though ambiguous, means at least more than half of the men. This means that the 'most men' in premise one must share at least one member with the 'most men' in premise two.*

Answers to Exercise 3.3

1. *Sound. The premises are true and the argument is valid.*

2. *Unsound. Although the argument is valid, and Darcey Bussell is indeed a ballet dancer, the first premise is false because men can be ballet dancers too.*

3. *Unsound. Although the premises are true the argument is invalid.*

4. *Unsound. Although the argument is valid the premises are false.*

5. *Unsound. Although the premises are true the argument is invalid.*

6. *Sound. The premises are true and the argument is valid.*

7. *Unsound. The first premise is false.*

8. *Sound. The premises are true and the argument is valid.*

9. *Unsound. The argument is invalid so we needn't consider whether most actors are talented or not.*

10. *Sound. The premises are true and the argument is valid.*

Answers to Exercise 3.4

1. *Deductive. A particular conclusion is derived from an assumed premise.*

2. *Inductive. The argument draws a general conclusion about Scottish football based on the observation of only one team.*

3. *Inductive. The argument makes a prediction about the future based on limited past experience.*

4. *Deductive. The argument draws a particular conclusion from an assumed general premise.*

5. *Inductive. The argument draws conclusions about other cats based on the observation of one cat.*

6. *Inductive. The argument draws a conclusion about all oysters based on a single experience of oysters in the past.*

7. *Deductive. The argument draws a conclusion about a specific dog based on an assumed premise concerning all dogs.*

8. *Inductive. The argument draws conclusions about the behaviour of water in one city based on past observations in another city.*

9. *Inductive. The argument draws conclusions about the past based on limited observations of the present.*

10. *Deductive. The argument reaches a conclusion about kumquats based on a general rule about citrus fruits.*

Answers to Exercise 3.5

1. *An invalid argument can have true premises – TRUE.*

2. *An invalid argument can have a true conclusion – TRUE.*

3. *An invalid argument can be sound – FALSE.*

4. *A valid argument can have true premises – TRUE.*

5. *A valid argument can have a false conclusion – TRUE.*

6. *A valid argument can have true premises and a false conclusion – FALSE.*

7. *A sound argument can have a false conclusion – FALSE (because the valid structure and true premises will always produce a true conclusion).*

8. *A sound argument can have a false premise – FALSE.*

9. *An unsound argument can have true premises and a true conclusion – TRUE (when it is invalid).*

10. *An unsound argument can be valid – TRUE (when one of its premises are false).*

Chapter 4

Showing the Structure of an Argument

Formal and Informal Methods

When faced with an ordinary language argument it is not always easy to see what is going on within the argument and so evaluate how well the argument works. A variety of methods or techniques can be used to help make the underlying structure of an argument more obvious. However, there is no one right method: each technique will focus on different aspects of the argument and show what is going on to varying degrees of detail. Moreover, different arguments will also lend themselves to some types of analysis more easily than others.

Some of these techniques can be classed as **formal methods** and some as **informal methods**. An informal method is one that simply shows how the premises and conclusions link together in a rough and ready way. For example, they may simply identify how many different premises and conclusions there are and put them in a logical sequence. **Argument diagrams** are a good example of an informal technique of showing argument form. This sort of informal technique is usually good enough for critical thinking.

More formal methods try to break into the structure of the premises to show how their component parts link together. **Set logic forms** and **statement logic forms** are good examples of more formal methods of laying out argument structures in a clear way. Some very technical methods like **predicate logic forms** represent the argument with what looks like mathematical symbols. This can be very intimidating to anyone who is new to critical thinking, but there is no need to learn every method of showing an argument's structure to be good at critical thinking. Such methods are usually reserved for the more technical study of formal logic. What is important for critical thinking is that we are able to show enough of what is going on to make a reasonable evaluation of how well an argument supports its conclusion.

A Comparison of Methods

Let's take an initial look at how each of these methods might analyse the same argument using the following ordinary language example:

- 'I think Rover is a carnivore. After all, he's a dog and all dogs are carnivores.'

One way of showing the structure of this argument would be to use an argument diagram, like so:

- $\underline{2 + 3}$ *1 = 'I think Rover is a carnivore'*
  $\downarrow$ *2 = 'Rover is a dog'*
  1   *3 = 'All dogs are carnivores'*

This basic method actually tells us a lot about the argument. It tells us that there are three distinct statements in the argument and that the first statement is in fact a conclusion, which is supported by the second and third statements, which are the premises. A set logic form, though, might give us a little more detail about this argument:

- All A are B   *A = Dogs*
  x is A   *B = Carnivores*
  x is B   *x = Rover*

This not only tells us that there are two premises and a conclusion, but also tells us something about what is going on *inside* these statements. The letters A and B represent the sets of 'Dogs' and 'Carnivores' respectively. This argument form says that all dogs are members of the set of carnivores and since Rover is a member of the set of dogs he must be a member of the set of carnivores too. This method has the added benefit of making it clearer why the argument is valid.

Statement logic forms are also an effective way of making the validity of this argument more obvious:

- If P then Q   *P = 'Rover is a dog'*
  $\underline{P}$ *Q = 'Rover is a carnivore'*
  Q

This method uses the letters P and Q to represent component statements of the argument, rather than sets of things. It depicts the argument as effectively saying: If Rover is a dog then he must be a carnivore; Rover is a dog; so he must be a carnivore. Again, the connection between the premises and the conclusion are made more explicit in this technique.

Each of these methods of depicting the structure of an argument is useful in its own way. However, it is important to remember that none of these methods is any more important than any other and that if you become comfortable with at least one method you will have a useful tool which will get you through most critical thinking examinations at this level.

Argument Diagrams

An argument diagram is an informal way of showing the structure of reasoning in an argument. Before you can produce an argument diagram for an ordinary language argument you need to do *four* things:

Creating an Argument Diagram

1. Circle any premise or conclusion indicator words.
2. Put brackets around each separate statement in the argument.
3. Number the statements. Statements that appear twice in the argument must use the same number.
4. Then use the numbers to diagram how the premises support the conclusion by joining these numbers together with arrows.

Some worked examples are shown below:

Example 1

- 'Today is either Thursday or Friday. But it can't be Friday because we get Philosophy on a Thursday and we are getting Philosophy today. So, it must be Thursday.'

Step 1: Circling the indicator words

- Today is either Thursday or Friday. But it can't be Friday because we get Philosophy on a Thursday and we are getting Philosophy today. So, it must be Thursday.

Step 2: Bracketing the statements

- (Today is either Thursday or Friday). But (it can't be Friday) because (we get Philosophy on a Thursday) and (we are getting Philosophy today). So, (it must be Thursday).

Step 3: Numbering the statements

- (Today is either Thursday or Friday)^1. But (it can't be Friday)^2 | because | (we only get Philosophy on a Thursday)^3 and (we are getting Philosophy today)^4. | So |, (it must be Thursday)^5.

Step 4: Showing how they link together

- $$\begin{array}{c} \underline{3 + 4} \\ \downarrow \\ \underline{1 + 2} \\ \downarrow \\ 5 \end{array}$$

This diagram is saying that statements 3 and 4 are premises for statement 2 and that statement 1 and 2 then in turn serve as premises for the conclusion, statement 5.

Example 2

- 'I am taller than you. After all, Peter is taller than Imran and Imran is taller than you. So, the fact that I am taller than Peter means I must be taller than you.'

Step 1: Circling the indicator words

- I am taller than you. | After all |, Peter is taller than Imran and Imran is taller than you. | So, the fact that | I am taller than Peter | means | I must be taller than you.

Step 2: Bracketing the statements

- (I am taller than you). | After all |, (Peter is taller than Imran) and (Imran is taller than you). | So, the fact that | (I am taller than Peter) | means | (I must be taller than you).

Step 3: Numbering the statements

- (I am taller than you)^1. | After all |, (Peter is taller than Imran)^2 and (Imran is taller than you)^3. | So, the fact that | (I am taller than Peter)^4 | means | (I must be taller than you)^1.

Step 4: Showing how they link together

- $\dfrac{4 + 2 + 3}{\downarrow}$

  1

Statements 4, 2 and 3 taken together lead to the conclusion, 1. Notice how the conclusion is repeated twice in the arguments, so on each occasion it is given the same number.

Example 3

- 'Craig can't be home because all the lights are out, there is a pile of unopened mail behind his letterbox and there are two weeks of milk deliveries on his doormat. No one leaves the lights out when they are home.'

Steps 1-3:

- (Craig can't be home)[1] because (all the lights are out)[2], (there is a pile of unopened mail behind his letterbox)[3] and (there are two weeks of milk deliveries on his doormat)[4]. (No one leaves the lights out when they are home)[5].

Step 4:

- $\underline{2 + 5}$ 3   4

  $\searrow$ $\downarrow$ $\swarrow$

  1

Statements 2 and 5 taken together lead to the conclusion, statement 1. However, statements 3 and 4 also provide independent reasons for supporting the conclusion without relying on each other. These premises on their own provide sufficient evidence for the conclusion so merit their own arrow pointing directly towards it.

Form and Content

Critical thinking is essentially an informal approach to argument evaluation so, on most occasions, argument diagrams are enough to identify the general structure of reasoning in an argument. However, occasionally we might wish to show how an argument works to a greater level of detail and to do this will require the use of more formal methods of setting out an argument's structure. **Set logic forms** and **statement logic forms** are two ways of doing this.

Before we outline how each of these methods work it is perhaps worth drawing an important distinction between the **form** of an argument and its **content**. The form of an argument is its underlying shape or structure while its content is its subject matter. Two arguments can share the same form but have very different content from one another. For example:

- All cows are herbivores
  Daisy is a cow
  Therefore, Daisy is an herbivore

- All cats are mammals
  Felix is a cat
  Therefore, Felix is a mammal

These arguments have very different content: one is about cows and the other is about cats. However, both of these arguments share a common structure or form which might be depicted like this:

- All A are B
  <u>x is A</u>
  x is B

How should we interpret these symbols? The words and letters in an argument form are known as the constants and variables. The letters 'A', 'B' and 'x' are the variables of this argument form while the words 'All', 'are' and 'is' are the constants. The line drawn between the premises and the conclusions stands for the word 'therefore'. To recreate the first argument the variable 'A' stands for cows; the variable 'B' stands for 'herbivores' and the variable 'x' stands for 'Daisy'. To recreate the second argument the variable 'A' stands for 'cats' the variable 'B' stands for 'mammals' and the variable 'x' stands for 'Felix'.

Formal methods are more precise than informal ones because they show what is going on *within* the component statements of the argument. Argument diagrams don't do this and so might make two arguments look similar in structure when in fact there might be significant differences. Consider the following two arguments:

- All cats are mammals
  Felix is a cat
  Therefore, Felix is a mammal

- All cats are mammals
  Felix is a mammal
  Therefore, Felix is a cat

Despite the fact that these two arguments are structurally different, argument diagrams could fail to show this difference:

- 1 + 2   *1 = All cats are mammals*
      ↓   *2 = Felix is a cat*
      3   *3 = Felix is a mammal*

- 1 + 2   *1 = All cats are mammals*
      ↓   *2 = Felix is a mammal*
      3   *3 = Felix is a cat*

However, using a more formal method, the argument could be depicted as having two distinct underlying forms:

- All A are B   *A = Cats*
  x is A   *B = Mammals*
  x is B   *x = Felix*

- All A are B   *A = Cats*
  x is B   *B = Mammals*
  x is A   *x = Felix*

These two forms might look similar but look again: the second form swaps the second premise with the conclusion. This makes a big difference because while the first argument has a valid form the second one has an invalid form. The more detailed our method of showing the form the easier it gets to understand where the second argument is going wrong.

Set Logic Forms

A set logic form is one where the variables of the form represent sets of things. Set logic forms show how these sets relate together within the argument. For example:

- All men are lazy
  Some men are Australian
  So, some Australians are lazy

Using set logic, this argument could be given the form:

- All A are B   *A = Men*
  Some A are C   *B = Lazy things*
  Some C are B   *C = Australians*

This argument has three sets ('Men', 'Lazy things' and 'Australians') and the form shows how these sets relate together. A common mistake is to think that the variables in this form stand for words and not sets, but the key that has been provided for this argument form makes it plain that this is not the case. The variable 'B' stands for the set of 'Lazy things' not the word 'Lazy'; the variable 'C' stands for the set of 'Australians', not the word 'Australian'.

If there were more sets we could go on adding more variables (e.g. D, E, etc.). Occasionally, however, we want to represent individuals as well as sets in an argument form. Consider the following argument:

- All men are lazy
  Brian is a man
  Therefore, Brian is lazy

This argument has only two sets ('Men' and 'Lazy things') and one individual ('Brian'). Brian is not a set but an individual so we use a small letter 'x' or 'y' to represent this individual rather than a capital 'A' or 'B'. The form of the argument might therefore be rendered thus:

- All A are B   *A = Men*
  x is A   *B = Lazy things*
  x is B   *x = Brian*

The constants in the above set logic form are the words 'all', 'are' and 'is', but a number of different constant terms can appear in set logic forms such as:

- All
- Some
- Most
- At least one
- Is
- Is not
- Are
- Are not

More examples of set logic forms are shown below:

- All dogs are dangerous   All A are B
  Fido is not dangerous   x is not B
  So, Fido is not a dog   x is not A

- Some cats are nervous   Some A are B
  All cats are mammals   All A are C
  So, some mammals are nervous Some C are B

- No rabbits are carnivorous   No A are B
  All carnivores are meat eaters All B are C
  So, no rabbits eat meat   No A are C

Statement Logic Forms

A statement logic form is one where the variables of the form represent statements rather than sets. Statement logic shows how these component statements link together within the argument. Statement logic is also sometimes referred to as **propositional logic**, because statements are also known by logicians as propositions. An example might be as follows:

- If you are Scottish then you are British
  You are Scottish
  Therefore, you are British

Although this argument is three sentences long it is actually composed of only two component statements: 'you are Scottish' and 'you are British', which reappear at various points in the argument.

- If [you are Scottish] then [you are British]
  [You are Scottish]
  Therefore, [you are British]

If we replace these statements with variables then we might see a different sort of underlying form. In statement logic, we use the letters P, Q and R as variables to avoid confusion with set logic, so the above argument might be rendered thus:

- If P then Q   *P = 'You are Scottish'*
  P   *Q = 'You are British'*
  Q

The constants in this argument form are the words 'if/then', but there are a number of words that can appear as constants in a statement logic form, such as:

- If/Then
- Or
- And
- Not
- If and only if

More examples of statement logic forms are shown below:

- Either you are Scottish or English   Either P or Q
  You are not English   Not Q
  So, you must be Scottish   P

- If you are human then you are a mammal   If P then Q
  Fish are not mammals   Not Q
  So, fish are not human   Not P

- I like chocolate   P
  I like ice cream   Q
  So, I like chocolate and ice cream   P and Q

Chapter Summary

- ✓ The underlying structure of an argument can be shown using a variety of methods: some formal and some informal.

- ✓ Informal methods simply identify the premises and conclusions in the argument and show their logical arrangement.

- ✓ Formal methods try to show what is going on *within* the premises and conclusions and so clarify how the component parts link together.

- ✓ Argument diagrams are one informal method for showing an argument's structure while set logic forms and statement logic forms are more formal methods for showing the underlying structure of an argument.

- ✓ Formal methods draw a distinction between the form and content of an argument.

- ✓ The form of an argument is its underlying structure while the content is its subject matter.

- ✓ Formal methods represent the form of an argument using a special notation composed of constants and variables.

- ✓ Constants are connective words (like 'and' or 'some') while variables are letters used as placeholders for sentences or words (like 'A' or 'B').

- ✓ Set logic forms use the variables A, B and C to represent sets within the argument and use constants like 'some', 'all' and 'no' to modify them.

- ✓ Statement logic forms use the variables P, Q and R to represent component statements within the argument and use constants like 'and', 'or' and 'if/then' as connectives.

Exercises

Answers to the following exercises can be found at the end of this chapter. If you have any difficulties with any of these questions refer back to the text of Chapter 4.

Exercise 4.1

Answer the following questions in your own words:

1. Name one informal technique for showing the structure of an argument.
2. Name one formal technique for showing the structure of an argument.
3. What is meant by the 'form' of an argument?
4. What is meant by the 'content' of an argument?
5. What is the difference between constants and variables in an argument form?
6. What letters are commonly used as variables in set logic forms?
7. What letters are commonly used as variables in statement logic forms?
8. What do the variables in set logic represent?
9. What do the variables in statement logic represent?
10. Why are formal methods better than informal methods for showing the structure of an argument?

Exercise 4.2

Show the structure of reasoning in the following arguments using an argument diagrams:

1. I don't like Peter so I'm not going to his party.
2. Gabriel gave a good interview. He also dressed very smartly. So, he should get the job.
3. I am a generous person! I gave my clothes to the Salvation Army. I also gave my watch to the PDSA and I gave my last fiver to the orphanage appeal fund.
4. If you eat before swimming you could get cramp and drown. So, if you have your lunch now you can't go to the swimming pool. You want to have your lunch now. Thus, you can't go to swimming afterwards.
5. Yesterday was Sunday. So, today must be Monday. The gallery is closed on

the first Monday of each month. Therefore, the gallery will be closed today.

6. If you had more money you could buy that jacket, but you don't so you can't.

7. I need to get some sleep. I've worked all day and I was awake all night.

8. He sent back the steak and didn't have any dessert. On balance, I don't think he thought much of the restaurant.

9. We must conclude that the aeroplane crashed because of pilot error. If he hadn't stalled the engine eight lives would have been saved.

10. Sheila is younger than Bruce and Bruce is 23. Greg is 25, so Sheila must be younger than Greg.

Exercise 4.3

In set logic the variables A, B and C are used to represent sets while the letters x and y are used to represent individuals. The constants in set logic are 'all', 'some', 'no', 'are', 'are not', 'is' and 'is not'. Hence, the sentence 'Some cats are not friendly' has the set logic form 'Some A are not B' (where A = cats and B = friendly things).

Show the underlying form of the following sentences using set logic forms. Remember to say what your variables stand for.

1. All men are irritable.

2. Some restaurants are expensive.

3. No women are easily fooled.

4. Some dogs are not dangerous.

5. No soldiers are not well fed.

6. Jack is happy.

7. The Prime Minister is not Tony Blair.

8. Sarah is not perfect.

9. Tehseen likes flowers.

10. Pedro hates Mondays.

Exercise 4.4

In statement logic the variables P, Q and R are used to represent statements. The constants in statement logic are 'And', 'Or', 'Not' and 'If/Then'. Hence, the sentence 'If you are Spanish then you are not Russian' has the statement logic form 'If P then not Q' (where P = 'you are Spanish' and Q = 'you are Russian').

Show the underlying form of the following sentences using statement logic forms. Remember to say what your variables stand for.

1. If you like music then you'll like Beethoven.

2. I am tired and I am hungry.

3. You're either a cat lover or you're a dog lover.

4. I am not rich.

5. If we buy our ticket now then we can go to the park and see the show.

6. You are not big or clever.

7. You either love football or you don't love football.

8. Tehseen likes flowers.

9. Peter likes football and tennis.

10. You either like tea but don't like coffee or you don't like tea but do like coffee.

Exercise 4.5

Show the underlying form of the following arguments using set logic forms. Remember to state what your variables stand for.

1. All tennis players are athletes
    No snooker players are athletes
    So, no tennis players are snooker players

2. All vegetables are nutritious
    Some vegetables are cheap
    Thus, some cheap things are nutritious

3. All budgies are birds
    Some birds are predators
    All budgies are predators

4. No women are reptiles
    Sabrina is not a reptile
    Thus, Sabrina is a woman

5. All postmen are efficient
    Some window cleaners are efficient
    Some window cleaners are postmen

Now show the underlying form of the following arguments using statement logic forms. Remember to state what your variables stand for.

6. I am poor
    I am honest
    Therefore, I am poor and I am honest

7. Either today is Wednesday or today is Thursday
    Today is not Wednesday
    So, today must be Thursday

8. If you are healthy then you are happy
    You are not healthy
    So, you are not happy

9. If you don't drink milk then you won't have strong bones
    You do have strong bones
    So, you do drink milk

10. If you go to the casino then you may lose all your money
    If you lose all your money then you will be unable to pay the rent
    So, if you go to the casino then you will be unable to pay the rent

Answers

Answers to Exercise 4.1

1. *Argument diagrams.*

2. *Either using Set Logic forms or using Statement Logic forms.*

3. *The form of an argument is its underlying structure or shape.*

4. *The content of an argument is its subject matter, what the argument is about.*

5. *The variables are placeholders for words or statements. The constants are connective words that join the variables together.*

6. *A, B and C are commonly used to represent sets while x and y are commonly used to represent individuals.*

7. *P, Q and R are commonly used to represent statements in statement logic.*

8. *The variables in sets logic represent groups or sets of things such as the set of dogs.*

9. *The variables in statement logic represent whole statement such as 'My dog is carnivorous.'*

10. *Formal methods are better than informal methods because they provide a greater level of detail about the structure of sentences in an argument and so are better able at revealing why an argument is valid or invalid.*

Answers to Exercise 4.2

1. *(I don't like Peter)[1]* $\boxed{\text{so}}$ *(I'm not going to his party)[2].*

    - 1
      ↓
      2

2. *(Gabriel gave a good interview.)[1] (He also dressed very smartly.)[2] So, (he should get the job.)[3]*

    - 1   2
       ↘ ↙
         3

3. *(I am a generous person!)[1] (I gave my clothes to the Salvation Army.)[2] (I*

also gave my watch to the PDSA)[3] and (I gave my last fiver to the orphanage appeal fund.)[4]

- 2   3   4
   ↘   ↓ ↙
         1

4. *(If you eat before swimming you could get cramp and drown.)[1] So, (if you have your lunch now you can't go to the swimming pool.)[2] (You want to have your lunch now.)[3] Thus, (you can't go to swimming afterwards.)[4]*

-      1
        ↓
      2 + 3
        ↓
        4

5. *(Yesterday was Sunday.)[1] So, (today must be Monday.)[2] (The gallery is closed on the first Monday of each month.)[3] Therefore, (the gallery will be closed today.)[4]*

-      1
        ↓
      2 + 3
        ↓
        4

6. *(If you had more money you could buy that jacket)[1], but (you don't)[2]* so *(you can't.)[3]*

- 1 + 2
    ↓
    3

7. *(I need to get some sleep.)[1] (I've worked all day)[2] and (I was awake all night.)[3]*

- 2   3
   ↘   ↙
      1

8.   *(He sent back the steak)[1] and (didn't have any dessert).[2] On* boxed *balance, (I don't think he thought much of the restaurant.)[3]*

- 1   2
  ↘   ↙
       3

9.   boxed *We must conclude that (the aeroplane crashed because of pilot error.)[1] (If he hadn't stalled the engine eight lives would have been saved.)[2]*

- 2
  ↓
  1

10. *(Sheila is younger than Bruce)[1] and (Bruce is 23.)[2] (Greg is 25)[3]* boxed *so (Sheila must be younger than Greg.)[4]*

- $\underline{1 + 2 + 3}$
  ↓
  4

Answers to Exercise 4.3

1.   *All A are B. (Where A = Men; B = Irritable things)*

2.   *Some A are B. (Where A = Restaurants; B = Expensive things)*

3.   *No A are B. (Where A = Women; B = Things which are easily fooled)*

4.   *Some A are not B. (Where A = Dogs; B = Dangerous things)*

5.   *No A are not B. (Where A = Soldiers; B = Well fed things)*

6.   *x is A. (Where x = Jack; B = Happy things)*

7.   *x is not y. (Where x = The Prime Minister; y = Tony Blair)*

8.   *x is not A. (Where x = Sarah; B = Perfect things)*

9.   *x is A. (Where x = Tehseen; A = Flower likers)*

10. *x is A. (Where x = Pedro; A = Monday haters)*

Answers to Exercise 4.4

1. *If P then Q. (Where P = 'You like music' and Q = 'You like Beethoven')*

2. *P and Q. (Where P = 'I am tired' and Q = 'I am hungry')*

3. *P or Q. (Where P = 'You are a cat lover' and Q = 'You are a dog lover')*

4. *Not P. (Where P = 'I am rich')*

5. *If P then Q and R. (Where P = 'If we buy our ticket now', Q = 'We can go to the park' and R = 'We can see the show')*

6. *Not P and not Q. (Where P = 'You are big' and Q = 'You are clever')*

7. *P or not P. (Where P = 'You love football')*

8. *P. (Where P = 'Tehseen likes flowers')*

9. *P and Q. (Where P = 'Peter likes football' and Q = 'Peter likes tennis')*

10. *(P and not Q) or (not P and Q). (Where P = 'You like tea' and Q = 'You like coffee')*

Answers to Exercise 4.5

1. *All A are B*
   No C are B
   No A are C

   (Where A = Tennis players, B = Athletes and C = Snooker players)

2. *All A are B*
   Some A are C
   Some C are B

   (Where A = Vegetables, B = Nutritious things and C = Cheap things)

3. *All A are B*
   Some B are C
   All A are C

   (Where A = Budgies, B = Birds and C = Predators)

4. *No A are B*
   x is not B
   x is A

   (Where A = Women, B = Reptiles and x = Sabrina)

71

5. *All A are B*
   Some B are C
   Some B are A

   (Where A = Postmen, B = Window cleaners and C = Efficient things)

6. *P*
   Q
   P and Q

   (Where P = 'I am Poor' and Q = 'I am honest')

7. *P or Q*
   Not P
   Q

   (Where P = 'Today is Wednesday' and Q = 'Today is Thursday')

8. *If P then Q*
   Not P
   Not Q

   (Where P = 'You are healthy' and Q = 'You are happy')

9. *If Not P then not Q*
   Q
   P

   (Where P = 'You drink milk' and Q = 'You have strong bones')

10. *If P then Q*
    If Q then R
    If P then R

    (Where P = 'You go to the casino', Q = 'You may lose all your money' and R = 'You will be unable to pay the rent')

Chapter 5

Testing Argument Validity

Some Informal Methods

How do we know when an argument is valid or invalid? How can we tell if it well structured or not? Our starting point should be our definition of validity: An argument is valid if it guarantees a true conclusion when the premises are true. With some arguments this definition is enough, by simply looking at the argument and imagining that the premises are true we can see whether the conclusion either does or doesn't follow from them[4]. However, some arguments are trickier and it isn't obvious whether the conclusion is necessitated by the premises. There are a number of techniques we can employ with varying degrees of success before we have to resort to more formal methods such as diagrams.

Intuition

Once we have assessed a large number of arguments we develop a knack at telling whether arguments are valid or invalid. We are able to see past the detail of the content and grasp almost by **intuition** whether an argument is well structured or not. However, no matter how honed our intuition is it will never safeguard us from making mistakes. This is because the validity or invalidity of some arguments is **counterintuitive**. For example, consider the following arguments:

1. All birds have feathers
    An eagle has feathers
    Therefore, an eagle is a bird

2. If it is raining then we're in Scotland
    We aren't in Scotland
    Therefore, it isn't raining

The first argument is intuitively convincing. All birds do indeed have feathers and an eagle is indeed a bird. However, the argument actually has an invalid structure or

---

[4] Remember we need only *imagine* that the premises are true, whether they are *in fact* true is only relevant to the soundness not the validity of the argument.

form. The second argument is intuitively unconvincing, but it actually has a valid form. These examples therefore demonstrate what an unreliable guide intuition can be.

Common Argument Forms

One of the reasons that we might be able to tell that the second argument is valid is because it has the valid form known as ***modus tollens***. This is any argument of the form:

- If P then Q
  Not Q
  Not P

It doesn't matter which words or statements P and Q stand for, we are always guaranteed that any argument with this shape is valid. By memorising this form we can spot it whenever it appears and so quickly state that the argument is valid without performing any calculation or deliberation at all. Another common valid form is ***modus ponens*** which is any argument of the form:

- If P then Q
  Not Q
  Not P

Again, whenever we identify any argument with this form we know straightaway that it must be valid. This suggests a strategy for identifying valid and invalid arguments: we could simply write down and memorise the most common argument forms, so enabling us to spot them whenever they arise.

This strategy is limited in use, however. Whilst many of the arguments we encounter do fall into common forms what would we do if we encountered an argument which had a form we had never encountered before?

Finding Counterexamples

Part of the reason that some arguments are difficult to assess is that we get distracted by the content of the argument and our prior knowledge of the world. In the two examples given at the outset of this chapter, we were distracted by our prior knowledge of birds and our prior knowledge of rain into an incorrect evaluation of the arguments. Had the arguments *not* had that particular content we would not have been so easily fooled. This suggests a third informal strategy for testing the validity of arguments: find another argument with the same form as the one under consideration, but with content that makes the validity or invalidity more explicit. For example:

- All birds have feathers
  An eagle has feathers
  Therefore, an eagle is a bird

This argument has the same form as this argument:

- All dogs have eyes
  A human being has eyes
  Therefore, a human being is a dog

However, this argument has two true premises followed by false conclusion which we know is an impossible state of affairs for a valid argument (since valid arguments guarantee true conclusion when the premises are true). This argument must therefore be invalid. Another example might be:

- If it is raining then we're in Scotland
  We aren't in Scotland
  Therefore, it isn't raining

This argument has the same form as the argument:

- If you are a dog then you are a mammal
  A lizard is not a mammal
  Therefore, a lizard is not a dog

This argument makes the validity more obvious. If all dogs are mammals then stands to reason that anything which isn't a mammal can't be a dog. Thus, by substituting the content of the argument with obviously true premises we have been able to make the evaluation of the argument easier. This method will only work if you ensure that the example you find has obviously true premises. However, this technique does require a bit of imagination and you will be at a loss if you cannot think of a suitable counterexample. This is why most logicians resort to more methodical approaches such as **Venn diagrams** and **truth tables**.

Venn Diagrams

Venn diagrams were invented by the mathematician **John Venn** (1834-1923). In mathematics they help map out the relationships between different sets of things, but in critical thinking they can be used to test the validity of set logic forms like 'All A are B, x is A, therefore x is B' (they cannot be used to test the validity of statement logic forms such as 'If P then Q, P therefore Q'). Venn diagrams are useful because they can help you depict what is going on in an argument in a visual way using circles. Since the human brain often handles pictures better than words or numbers, they can sometimes show what is wrong with an argument more quickly than other methods.

In Venn diagrams we draw a circle for each set that we want to represent. If there is only one set we draw one circle; if there are two sets we draw two circles; if there are three sets we draw three circles, and so on. The more circles we draw, the more areas we delineate. For example, look at the one circle Venn diagram below which represents the set of birds. How many different areas does it delineate?

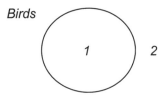

The answer is that it marks out two distinct areas: the area inside the circle and the area outside the circle. If this circle represents the set of birds then that means that anything that is a bird (such as parrots, sparrows and pigeons) can be placed inside the circle, and anything which isn't a bird (such as cats, dogs and humans) must be placed outside the circle.

In a two circle Venn we can delineate four areas. This might seem surprising but let's look at an example. Imagine we wanted to represent the set of birds and the set of females on the same diagram. We would draw the diagram like so:

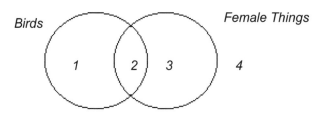

The two intersecting circles create three distinct areas and if we count the area outside of the circles as part of the diagram that makes four areas in total. What should become apparent is that each of these four areas represents a different group of things. In this example these would be:

- Section 1: Birds that aren't female.
- Section 2: Birds that are female.
- Section 3: Females that aren't birds.
- Section 4: Everything which is neither a bird nor female.

In a three circle Venn diagram, there are even more areas because three intersecting circles create eight distinct segments. An example showing the intersecting sets of mammals, cats and males is shown below:

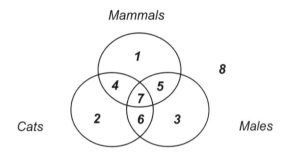

- Section 1: Mammals which aren't cats or male.
- Section 2: Cats which aren't male or mammals.
- Section 3: Males which aren't cats or mammals.
- Section 4: Cats which are mammals but aren't male.
- Section 5: Mammals which are male but not cats.
- Section 6: Cats which are male but not mammals.
- Section 7: Cats which are male and mammals.
- Section 8: Everything which isn't a cat or a mammal or male.

Of course not all of these sections will necessarily have any members: there is such a thing as an 'empty set'. The set of 'Cats which aren't mammals' might be an example of an empty set.

Now the curious thing about Venn diagrams is that *every object in the universe can be depicted on any Venn diagram no matter what it is about*. This might sound incredible but Kylie Minogue, for example, could be placed in section 3 and an electric kettle could be placed in section 4. There is even a place for you on this diagram! In fact, it is impossible to think of an object which doesn't have a place in this diagram. This is even more remarkable when you consider that this isn't just true of this particular diagram, but is true of *any* Venn diagram you care to draw. This is what makes Venn diagrams an immensely powerful tool.

Representing Statements with Venn Diagrams

Before we can look at how Venn diagrams can depict a whole argument we need to learn how to represent individual statements with a diagram. To simplify matters we will limit the range of statements to four main types:

- Statements about individuals, such as 'Polly is a bird.'
- 'All' statements, such as 'All birds are feathered.'
- 'No' statements, such as 'No birds are feathered.'
- 'Some' statements, such as 'some birds are feathered.'

Depicting Individuals with a Venn Diagram

Let's begin with the statement 'Polly is a bird.' This statement only contains one set: the set of birds (Polly is an individual and individuals are not sets). So, to diagram this statement we only need one circle which we will label 'birds'. We will then depict Polly with the letter 'p' and put this letter inside the set of birds to show that Polly is a member of that set like so:

- 'Polly is a Bird'

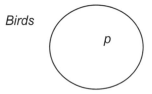

To represent the statement 'Polly is not a bird' we would have to place the letter 'p' outside the circle like so:

- 'Polly is not a Bird'

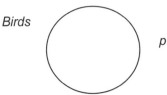

Depicting 'All' Statements with a Venn Diagram

If a statement contains more than one set then we will need more than one circle. For example, the statement 'All birds are feathered' involves two sets, so requires two circles. When depicting statements which concern more than one set, we always draw the circles intersecting and shade out the areas that we don't need.

- 'All birds are feathered'

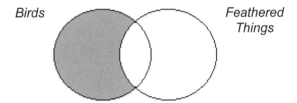

Notice how the section on the left has been shaded out. In Venn diagrams we shade out sections to indicate that they are empty. This diagram is trying to represent the statement that 'All birds are feathered', but since the section on the left is the area representing birds which aren't feathered we must shade this out to show it has no members. This means that the only segment of the set of birds remaining is the middle oval-shaped section and since this segment is entirely within the set of feathered things, the diagram clearly shows that all birds are feathered.

Depicting 'No' Statements with a Venn Diagram

If our statement had claimed that 'No birds are feathered' rather than 'All birds are feathered' it would have required a slightly different diagram. Again the statement would have required two circles because it concerns two sets. But we would need to shade out a different area of the diagram:

- 'No birds are feathered'

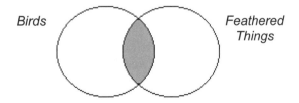

Notice how the middle section has been shaded out in this case. This is because this middle section represents those birds which are also feathered. This must be an empty set if the claim that 'No birds are feathered' is true.

Depicting 'Some' Statements with a Venn Diagram

The word 'some' in the English language is slightly ambiguous and is therefore harder to represent in a diagram. If you say you have 'some money' it could mean you have a penny or it could mean you are a millionaire. Therefore, in depicting the word 'some' in a Venn diagram we must adopt an agreed definition that 'some' means 'at least one'. To show that a set has some members we put an 'x' in the circle to show that it has at least one member. The statement 'Some birds are feathered' could therefore be depicted like so:

- 'Some birds are feathered'

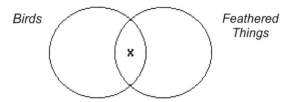

The 'x' goes in the middle because this section contains the set of birds which are also feathered which the statement claims has at least one member. The statement 'Some birds are not feathered' could be depicted like so:

- 'Some birds are not feathered'

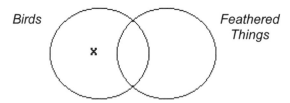

This diagram is saying that there is at least one non-feathered bird, which is the same as saying that 'Some birds are not feathered.'

Testing Argument Validity using Venn Diagrams

Now that we have learned how to depict a range of different statements using Venn diagrams we can use this knowledge to test the validity of a number of arguments. The process for doing this involves the following four steps:

Creating a Venn Diagram

1. Start by drawing a circle for every set in the argument. Give each circle an appropriate label.
2. Then depict each of the premises of the argument one at a time on the same diagram. Don't depict the conclusion, however.
3. Once you have depicted every premise, look at the diagram carefully.
4. If the argument is valid the conclusion *should already be evident on your diagram.* If the argument is invalid, *you will not be able to see the conclusion in the diagram.*

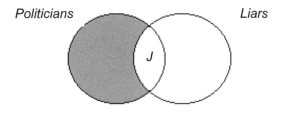

It might seem remarkable that by simply depicting the premises of a valid argument on a diagram we can simply read off the conclusion. However, this fact should be obvious once we appreciate that in a valid argument the conclusion is already *contained* in the premises. Let's test this out with some examples.

Example 1

Consider the following argument:

- All politicians are liars
  Mr Jones is a politician
  So, Mr Jones is a liar

81

Step 1: Draw and label a circle for each set

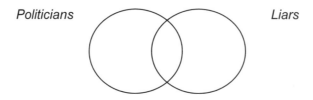

This argument contains two sets: the set of politicians and the set of liars. Mr Jones isn't a set but an individual, so we will only require two sets.

Step 2: Depict each of the premises on the diagram

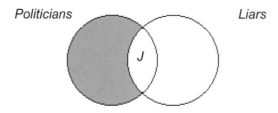

This argument has two premises. The first premise says 'All politicians are liars', so to represent this we will shade out the left hand section of the diagram so that the only politicians remaining are within the set of liars. We then must depict the second premise that 'Mr Jones is a politician.' Now, we could have put Mr Jones in the left hand section of the diagram, but the first premise has told us that this segment is empty because it is shaded out. We therefore have no choice but to put him in the middle section of the diagram because this is the only area of politicians left.

Steps 3 and 4: Assessing the diagram

We should now look at the diagram carefully and ask ourselves if the conclusion can read off from what we have already drawn. The conclusion states that 'Mr Jones is a liar' and if we look at our diagram we can see that Mr Jones, represented by the letter 'J', is indeed within the set of liars. This means that this argument is valid.

Example 2

Consider this next argument:

- All sea captains are sailors
  Bert is a sailor
  So, Bert is a sea captain

Step 1: Draw and label a circle for each set

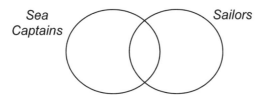

Again this is an argument with only two sets, so it only requires a two-circle Venn.

Step 2: Depict each of the premises on the diagram

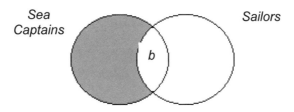

The first premise is easy enough: 'All sea captains are sailors' requires us to shade out the area representing sea captains who aren't sailors in the left hand segment. The second premise is more problematic though. If we are told that Bert is a sailor then there are two possible places to put him: either in the middle segment where he would be a sailor and a sea captain or in the right hand segment where he would be a sailor who isn't a sea captain. At present we don't have enough information to say for certain which area he belongs to so for the time being we will put him on the line which separates the two areas.

Steps 3 and 4: Assessing the diagram

Can we read off the conclusion 'Bert is a sea captain' from this diagram? The answer is that we can't. While it is *possible* that Bert is a sea captain we are not *guaranteed* that this is the case using the premises provided and the definition of a valid argument is that it must guarantee a true conclusion when the premises are true. This means that the argument must be invalid.

Example 3

Now let's consider an example of an argument which uses three sets:

- All politicians are liars
  No liars are trustworthy
  So, no politicians are trustworthy

Step 1: Draw and label a circle for each set

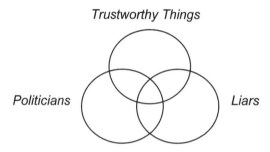

Since the argument refers to three distinct sets we will require three interlocking circles.

Step 2: Depict each of the premises on the diagram

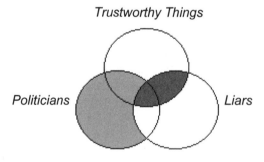

Shading three-circle Venn diagrams is a little trickier. The first premise says that all politicians are liars so we must shade out any part of the politicians set that isn't within the set of liars. The second premise then tells us that no liars are trustworthy so we must shade out any areas which could contain trustworthy liars. This section has been shaded in a darker colour to make it easier to see.

Steps 3 and 4: Assessing the diagram

Can we read off the conclusion 'No politicians are trustworthy' from this diagram? In this case we can because the only remaining unshaded part of the set of politicians is not within the set of trustworthy things. Hence the argument is valid.

Example 4

This final example involves a more complex three-circle Venn. Consider the following argument:

- All philosophers are wise
  Some vegetarians are wise
  So, some vegetarians are philosophers

The first premise states that all philosophers are wise which means that we must shade out any areas which could contain unwise philosophers. The second premise tells us that some vegetarians are wise so we know there is at least one wise vegetarian. However, we do not know for certain whether our wise vegetarian should be placed in the philosopher set or outside of it. We have no option therefore but to place it on the border between these two possibilities. This means that the argument is invalid because we are not guaranteed that some vegetarians must be philosophers.

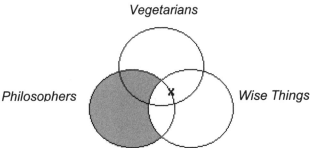

Limitations of Venn Diagrams

Using the techniques described above, it is possible to test the validity of a small range of simple arguments with a Venn diagram. However, we must be aware that formal methods like Venn diagrams are necessarily limited in the range of arguments they can cope with. For example, the diagrams above can only deal with four types of statement. They cannot cope with statements like 'Most men are wise' or deal satisfactorily with certain types of existential statements such as 'Tony Blair exists.' To deal with these sorts of statement would require more sophisticated sorts of diagram and there are plenty of books available which go into Venn theory in more depth than we have covered here. However, even these more sophisticated methods will break down once we get into more complex arguments involving five or six different sets.

Truth Tables

Truth tables are another formal method for testing argument validity. A truth table is a way of mapping out all the possible truth combinations within an argument to reveal whether any invalid truth combinations could arise. While Venn diagrams analyse an argument in terms of the sets within the argument, truth tables analyse arguments in terms of their component statements. So, in other words, truth tables can only be used to test the validity of statement logic forms like 'If P then Q, P therefore Q' (they cannot be used to test the validity of set logic forms such as 'All A are B, x is A, therefore x is B').

A truth table looks like this:

Variables		Premise 1	Premise 2	Conclusion
P	**Q**	**P → Q**	**P**	**Q**
T	T	T	T	T
T	F	F	T	F
F	T	T	F	T
F	F	T	F	F

Don't worry if this looks a little scary, the section below will explain how to create and interpret these tables. Before we can create truth tables to test the validity of whole arguments, though, we need to learn how to create truth tables for the component statements in an argument. As we did in our treatment of Venn diagrams, we will limit the range of statements to four main types:

- 'And' statements, such as 'I have brown hair and I've been to China.'
- 'Or' statements such as 'I have brown hair or I've been to China.'
- 'If/then' statements, such as 'If you are French then you will like onion soup.'
- 'Not' statements, such as 'London is not in Germany.'

Depicting 'And' Statements with a Truth Table

'And' statements are just any statement with the word 'and' in them. In logic, 'and' statements are known as **conjunctions**. Conjunctions actually contain two separate statements which have been 'glued' together with the word 'and'. For example:

- '<u>I have brown hair</u> **and** <u>I have been to China.</u>'

This sentence joins the statement 'I have brown hair' to the statement 'I have been to China.' If we use the variables P and Q to represent the component statements, we can see that all conjunctions have the underlying form:

- P and Q

In most logic books, the word 'and' is replaced with the symbol '&' for quickness so the form is usually written:

- P & Q

Given that conjunctions have two halves, each of which is capable of being true or false, there will be four different truth combinations possible for 'and' statements. Either P and Q are both true; or P is true while Q is false; or P is false while Q is true; or P and Q are both false. We can therefore produce a truth table which shows all these possible truth combinations.

It is very important that you fill out the P and Q columns in exactly the same pattern every time you create a truth table. If you don't your truth table will still work, but it will make it difficult to check your truth table with other people or with the answers at the end of the chapter. If you look at the innermost column the pattern is always alternating T's and F's (TFTF). If you now look at the column to the left of it the pattern is always two T's and two F's (TTFF). By following this pattern you will ensure that when you read the rows horizontally that you will get every possible combination of truth and falsity for two variables (TT, TF, FT and FF):

P	Q	P & Q
T	T	
T	F	
F	T	
F	F	

To complete the table we have to consider what effect these truth values have on the truth value of the statement as a whole. For example, if it is true that I have brown hair, and it is true that I have been to China, then my composite claim that 'I have brown hair and I've been to China' is true. If it is true that I have brown hair but false that I've been to China then my claim that 'I have brown hair *and* I've been to China' is false. If we go through this process for every truth combination then the completed truth table for 'and' statements looks like this:

P	Q	P & Q
T	T	T
T	F	F
F	T	F
F	F	F

Study the third column of this table carefully. What it is saying is that 'and' statements are always false except when P and Q are both true. In other words, if any part of a conjunction is false, the whole statement becomes false. This is quite a startling discovery because this is not just true of the particular statement that we have been looking at, but is true of every 'and' statement that will ever be uttered by a human being. Think about this the next time you ask your partner where they were last night. If they say 'I was at the cinema *and* I was watching a film' then a quick consultation of this truth table will reveal that there are more ways for them to be lying than for them to be telling the truth!

Depicting 'Or' Statements with a Truth Table

'Or' statements function in a similar way to 'And' statements in that they glue together two component statements with the word 'or'. In logic these statements are known as **disjunctions**. However, the truth table for disjunctions is very different from the truth table for conjunctions. An example might be:

- 'I have brown hair **or** I have been to China.'

This has the underlying form:

- P or Q

In some logic books this will be written as:

- P v Q

The truth table for 'or' statements is as follows:

P	Q	P v Q
T	T	T
T	F	T
F	T	T
F	F	F

Examine this table closely. What it is telling us is that sentences with the word 'or' in them are almost always true except when both P and Q are false. If it is true that I have brown hair but false that I've been to China, then my claim that 'I have brown hair or I have been to China' is still true. In order for the statement 'I have brown hair or I have been to China' to be true we only need one half of the statement to be true, but if both halves are false then the whole statement is false. This means there are more ways for 'or' statements to be true than there are for 'and' statements to be true.

The Inclusive and Exclusive use of 'Or'

We must be careful, however, when we define words in the English language by means of a truth table. This is because some words in the English language have more than one meaning. The word 'or' is a case in point. In some contexts it can mean 'one or the other or both' and in other contexts it can mean 'one or the other but *not* both.' For example, compare the following two sentences:

1. 'The successful candidate will have a degree *or* considerable work experience.'

2. 'The lunchtime special menu includes a starter and main course *or* a main course and a dessert.'

The first sentence is using 'or' in the sense of 'one or other or both.' Presumably a candidate would not be disqualified for being a graduate *and* having work experience. The second sentence is using 'or' in the sense of 'one or other but not both. The restaurant wouldn't want you to have all three courses in the lunchtime special. This first use is known as the **inclusive use of 'or'** while the second use is known as the **exclusive use of 'or'**. Each of these uses of the word 'or' will have a different effect on the truth value of statements in which they appear so each use will require a different truth table. The truth table above is the truth table for the inclusive use of or and for the sake of simplicity we will always assume that 'or' is intended in this inclusive sense to mean 'one or other or both.'

Depicting 'If/Then' Statements with a Truth Table

'If/then' statements are known as **implications**. An example might be:

- 'If you <u>are French</u> **then** <u>you will like onion soup</u>.'

Such statements have the form:

- If P then Q

An arrow symbol is often used to indicate the 'if/then' relationship like so:

- $P \rightarrow Q$

The truth table for 'if/then' statements is as follows:

P	Q	$P \rightarrow Q$
T	T	T
T	F	F
F	T	T
F	F	T

Imagine someone made the prediction: 'If you are French then you will like onion soup.' In order to test this theory you might start asking people whether they like onion soup or not. If you find a French person who *does* like onion soup then this will confirm the prediction, so generating the first line of our truth table. Because this person is French and likes onion soup, both halves of the implication are true and this will make the whole statement true. If, however, you find someone who is French but *doesn't* like onion soup then this makes that prediction false, so generating the second line of our truth table.

The remaining two lines of the truth table are a little trickier to grasp. If we find a person who isn't French but *does* like onion soup then this might at first seem to falsify our prediction. However, the prediction only claims that 'If you are French then you will like onion soup', it does not claim that '*Only* French people like onion soup.' This means that we haven't contradicted our prediction and so justifies the third line of our table. Finally, a person who is not French and doesn't like onion soup cannot falsify our prediction either because our prediction only concerns French people and claims nothing about people from other countries. This is why two falses make a true in the fourth line of our table.

Depicting 'Not' Statements with a Truth Table

'Not' statements are slightly different from all the other examples we have looked at so far. 'Not' statements, also known as **negations**, don't 'glue' two component statements together: they simply negate or deny the truth of a single statement. For example:

- 'London is **not** in Germany'

This sentence merely denies or negates the statement 'London is in Germany' and is the same as saying 'Not (London is in Germany).' The form of this statement is therefore:

- Not P

Or to use conventional notation:

- ~ P

The wavy line in front of the P is known as a **'tild'**, which is sometimes used in preference to a minus sign which has mathematical connotations (subtracting something isn't the same as denying it). Because 'not' statements normally only contain one statement, they have only two possible combinations of truth and falsity. If P is true then not P will be false and if P is false, not P will be true.

P	~ P
T	F
F	T

For example, if I say 'London is not in Germany' then, because the statement 'London is in Germany' is false, my negating it produces a true statement. Similarly, if I say 'London is not in England' then, because the statement 'London is in England' is true, my negating it will produce a false statement. It is worth pointing out that the English language has many ways of expressing a negation other than explicitly using the word 'not'. For example:

- 'It is false that I like onion soup.'
- 'I don't like onion soup.'
- 'It is erroneous to assert that I like onion soup.'

All of these sentences have the underlying form '~ P'.

91

Testing Argument Validity using Truth Tables

We have now produced four truth tables which show all the possible truth permutations for four types of statement.

P	Q	P & Q
T	T	T
T	F	F
F	T	F
F	F	F

P	Q	P v Q
T	T	T
T	F	T
F	T	T
F	F	F

P	Q	P → Q
T	T	T
T	F	F
F	T	T
F	F	T

P	~ P
T	F
F	T

Each of these component tables tells us a universal law which holds for all statements of that type:

- 'And' statements always false except when both P and Q are true.
- 'Or' statements are always true except when both P and Q are false.
- 'If/then' statements are always true except when P is true and Q is false.
- 'Not' statements always reverse the truth value of P.

We can now use these tables to generate more complex tables for testing the validity of whole arguments.

The process for doing this involves the following steps:

Creating a Truth Table

1. First, write down the underlying statement logic form of the argument.
2. Then create a column for each variable in the argument.
3. Now add a column for each of the premises and the conclusion.
4. Fill in the truth values for the variable columns.
5. Then calculate the truth values for the remaining columns.
6. Once you have completed each column, look at the diagram carefully.
7. If the argument is valid then *every* row where the premises are true should always show a true conclusion.

Variables		Premise 1	Premise 2	Conclusion
P	Q	P → Q	P	Q
T	T	T	T	T
T	F	F	T	F
F	T	T	F	T
F	F	T	F	F

92

Now let's see truth tables in action with some worked examples.

Example 1

- Either you are rich or you are honest
  You are not rich
  So, you must be honest

This argument has the underlying form:

- P or Q
  Not P
  Q

There are only two variables in this argument: P and Q. P stands for the statement 'You are rich' and Q stands for the statement 'You are honest.' Because there are only two variables there are only four possible truth combinations which we will insert into our table:

Variables		Premise 1	Premise 2	Conclusion
P	Q	P v Q	~ P	Q
T	T			
T	F			
F	T			
F	F			

We can now calculate the truth values for the first premise. We do this by referring back to the component truth tables we created earlier. These tell us that 'or' statements are always true except when P and Q are both false. Check the previous page if you need to remind yourself what the truth table for 'or' statements looks like.

Variables		Premise 1	Premise 2	Conclusion
P	Q	P v Q	~ P	Q
T	T	T		
T	F	T		
F	T	T		
F	F	F		

Premise 2 says 'Not P' so is the opposite of the values we have for P in the variable column. The conclusion Q can be directly copied from the values we have in the Q variable column.

Variables		Premise 1	Premise 2	Conclusion
P	**Q**	**P v Q**	**~ P**	**Q**
T	T	T	F	T
T	F	T	F	F
F	T	T	T	T
F	F	F	T	F

With our truth table complete we must now interpret it to see if the argument is valid or invalid. Our definition of validity is that valid arguments *guarantee* a true conclusion when all of the premises are true. Now, if we look at the truth table above we will see that there is only one occasion when all the premises are true and this is on row three of the table. In row three our two true premises have produced a true conclusion. This means that we are always guaranteed a true conclusion when the premises are true and that the argument is therefore valid.

Valid

Variables		Premise 1	Premise 2	Conclusion
P	**Q**	**P v Q**	**~ P**	**Q**
T	T	T	F	T
T	F	T	F	F
F	T	T	T	T
F	F	F	T	F

The beauty of truth tables is that they not only test the validity of a particular argument, but they also show that *any* argument which shares that form is also invalid. This means that if we encounter an argument which has the same form but completely different content, we don't need to create another truth table to test its validity since we have already tested the validity of all possible arguments which share that form.

Example 2

- If you are Swiss then you will like skiing
  You are not Swiss
  So, you won't like skiing

This argument has the underlying form:

- If P then Not Q
  Q
  Not P

There are only two variables in this argument: P and Q. P stands for the statement 'You are Swiss' and Q stands for the statement 'You will like skiing.' Because there are only two variables there are only four possible truth combinations which we will insert into our table:

Variables		Premise 1	Premise 2	Conclusion
P	**Q**	**P → Q**	**~ P**	**~ Q**
T	T			
T	F			
F	T			
F	F			

We can now calculate the truth values for the first premise. We do this by referring back to the component truth tables we created earlier. These tell us that if/then statements are always true except when P is true and Q is false.

Variables		Premise 1	Premise 2	Conclusion
P	**Q**	**P → Q**	**~ P**	**~ Q**
T	T	T		
T	F	F		
F	T	T		
F	F	T		

The second premise is a little trickier. It says 'Not P' so this column must be the *opposite* of whatever we have put in the P variable column. So too with the conclusion: it says 'Not Q' so we must fill that column with the *opposite* of whatever we have in the Q variable column. These columns have been completed in the table below:

Variables		Premise 1	Premise 2	Conclusion
P	**Q**	**P → Q**	**~ P**	**~ Q**
T	T	T	F	F
T	F	F	F	T
F	T	T	T	F
F	F	T	T	T

We are now ready to analyse our completed truth table. Remember, definition of validity is that valid arguments *guarantee* a true conclusion when all of the premises are true. In this table there are two occasions when all of the premises are true: row three *and* row four. If we now look at the truth value for the conclusion in row three we can see that the two premises have indeed produced a true conclusion. However, row four produces a false conclusion from true premises so we are not guaranteed a true conclusion from true premises on *every occasion* and this means that this argument must be invalid.

Invalid

Variables		Premise 1	Premise 2	Conclusion
P	**Q**	**P → Q**	**~ P**	**~ Q**
T	T	T	F	T
T	F	F	F	F
F	T	T	T	T
F	F	T	T	F

Example 3

- If you have small children then you wouldn't buy a snake
  You bought a snake
  So, you can't have small children

This argument has the underlying form:

- If P then Not Q
  Q
  Not P

Again there are only two variables in this argument and we can fill in the truth values accordingly:

Variables		Premise 1	Premise 2	Conclusion
P	**Q**	**P → ~ Q**	**Q**	**~ P**
T	T			
T	F			
F	T			
F	F			

The first premise of this argument is more difficult than those in our previous examples. This is because it contains more than one variable: 'If/then' and 'Not'. This means that we need to work out the truth values for each half of the if/then statement before we can calculate its collective truth value. 'P' is easy to calculate since we can simply copy those values from the P variable column. 'Not Q' requires us to invert the truth values in the Q column:

Variables		Premise 1		Premise 2	Conclusion
P	Q	P →	~ Q	Q	~ P
T	T	T	F		
T	F	T	T		
F	T	F	F		
F	F	F	T		

Now we have these values we can work out the collective value of the whole statement 'If P then not Q'. To do this we apply the rule for if/then statements which is that if/then statements are always true except when P is true and Q is false.

Variables		Premise 1			Premise 2	Conclusion
P	Q	P	→	~ Q	Q	~ P
T	T	T	F	F		
T	F	T	T	T		
F	T	F	T	F		
F	F	F	T	T		

Once we calculate the truth values for the first premise we no longer require the truth values that we calculate for each half of the if/then statement (these were just a stepping stone to help us arrive at truth values for the whole statement). We can now fill in the remaining columns. Premise 2 is a straightforward copy from the Q variable column and the conclusion is simply the opposite of the P variable column.

Valid

Variables		Premise 1	Premise 2	Conclusion
P	Q	P → ~ Q	Q	~ P
T	T	F	T	F
T	F	T	F	F
F	T	T	T	T
F	F	T	F	T

An analysis of this table reveals that we only have true premises on one occasion and this is in row three. Moreover, row three also provides a true conclusion which means that we are always guaranteed a true conclusion when the premises are true, thus demonstrating that this argument is valid.

Limitations of Truth Tables

Using the techniques described above, it is possible to test the validity of a range of simple arguments with a truth table. However, truth tables, like Venn diagrams, also have their limitations. For example, how do we test the validity of arguments with more than two variables? In order to do this we need a bigger truth table. A statement or argument with one variable only needs to be two rows high because there are only two possible truth combinations for one variable: true or false. The truth table for such a statement might look like this:

P	P v ~P
T	
F	

A statement or argument with two variables will require a table that is four rows high because there are four different truth combinations. For example:

P	Q	P → Q
T	T	
T	F	
F	T	
F	F	

Once we add a third variable things start to get complicated because we now need eight rows to cover all the possible truth combinations: that's double the amount we needed for a two variable statement. For example:

P	Q	R	P → Q v R
T	T	T	
T	T	F	
T	F	T	
T	F	F	
F	T	T	
F	T	F	
F	F	T	
F	F	F	

Notice the pattern of T's and F's in this three variable truth table. The innermost column for the 'R' variable still has the same pattern as all our previous innermost columns: alternating T's and F's (TFTFTFTF). The next column for the variable Q, has a pattern of two T's and two F's (TTFFTTFF) and the final column has four T's followed by four F's (TTTTFFFF). Each row we add doubles the number of T's and F's. Remember sticking to this same pattern of T's and F's with every truth table we make guarantees that when we read the table horizontally we will have covered every possible truth combination for three variables (TTT, TTF, TFT, TFF, FTT, FTF, FFT and FFF).

If we had four variables we would need 16 rows, five would require 32 rows and so on. In other words, every time we add a variable we need to double the size of the truth table. This means that there is a practical limit to the complexity of arguments that truth tables can deal with. Once we get to arguments with more than say four variables we could really do with a computer to work out all the possible truth values.

Another limitation of truth tables is the number of constants they can deal with. For the sake of simplicity we have looked at truth tables that can cope with four different constants: 'And', 'Or', 'If/then' and 'Not'. However, there are a number of other connectives that we could have included such as 'if and only if' and the exclusive use of 'or' (this has a different truth table from the inclusive use or 'or' which we have been using.) If we came across any other constants we would need to further complicate our system to accommodate them and again this imposes another practical limitation on the number of arguments we can evaluate just using a pencil and paper.

Chapter Summary

✓ Intuition is an unreliable guide to assessing whether an argument is valid or not because some valid arguments appear invalid and vice versa.

✓ One informal method of identifying invalid arguments is by thinking of counter examples which have the same structure as the argument under consideration, but produce a false conclusion from true premises.

✓ Another informal method is to memorise common valid and invalid forms to enable us to identify them whenever they arise.

✓ More formal and reliable methods of assessing argument validity include Venn diagrams and truth tables.

✓ Venn diagrams can be used to test the validity of set logic forms while truth tables can be used to test the validity of statement logic forms.

✓ A Venn diagram reveals that an argument is valid when the conclusion can be read from a diagram of the premises.

✓ A truth table reveals that an argument is valid if on every occasion where the premises are true the conclusion is also always true.

✓ Both Venn diagrams and truth tables are limited in the range of arguments they can deal with by the number of different constants and variables they can depict.

Exercises

Answers to the following exercises can be found at the end of this chapter. If you have any difficulties with any of these questions refer back to the text of Chapter 5.

Exercise 5.1

Answer the following questions in your own words:

1. Provide one example of a common argument form which is valid.

2. What do the circles represent in a Venn diagram?

3. What does a shaded circle indicate in a Venn diagram?

4. What does the symbol 'x' signify in a Venn diagram?

5. When would a Venn diagram indicate that an argument is valid?

6. In what circumstances are 'and' statements true?

7. In what circumstances are 'if/then' statements false?

8. What is the difference between the inclusive and exclusive uses of the word 'or'?

9. When would a truth table indicate that an argument is valid?

10. Why are Venn diagrams and truth tables limited in their usefulness?

Exercise 5.2

Depict the following sentences with a Venn diagram:

1. Jack is happy.

2. The Prime Minister is not a Liberal Democrat.

3. Sarah is not perfect.

4. Tehseen likes flowers.

5. Pedro hates Mondays.

6. All men are irritable.

7. Some restaurants are expensive.

8. No women are easily fooled.

9. Some dogs are not dangerous.

10. No soldiers are not well fed.

Exercise 5.3

Test the validity of the following arguments using Venn diagrams:

1. All thoughtful people are good friends
   Ahmed is a thoughtful person
   Therefore, Ahmed is a good friend

2. No clever people are lazy
   Jade is clever
   So, Jade is not lazy

3. All painters are artists
   All artists are talented
   So, all painters are talented

4. No men are fish
   No fish are architects
   So, no men are architects

5. Some doctors are good listeners
   Some good listeners are deaf
   Hence, some doctors are deaf

6. All tennis players are athletes
   No snooker players are athletes
   So, no tennis players are snooker players

7. All vegetables are nutritious
   Some vegetables are cheap
   Thus, some cheap things are nutritious

8. All budgies are birds
   Some birds are predators
   All budgies are predators

9. No women are reptiles. Sabrina is not a reptile. Thus, Sabrina is a woman.

10. All postmen are efficient. Some window cleaners are efficient. So, some window cleaners are postmen.

Exercise 5.4

Create truth tables for the following statements:

1. If you like music then you'll like Beethoven.
2. I am tired and I am hungry.
3. You're either a cat lover or you're a dog lover.
4. I am not rich.
5. If we buy our ticket now we can go to the park and see the show.
6. To be or not to be.
7. You are not big or clever.
8. Tehseen likes flowers.
9. Peter likes football and tennis.
10. You either like tea but don't like coffee or you don't like tea but do like coffee.

Exercise 5.5

Test the validity of the following arguments using truth tables:

1. I am poor
    I am honest
    Therefore, I am poor and I am honest

2. If the budget is favourable we'll pay less tax
    The budget was favourable
    So, we'll pay less tax

3. Either today is Wednesday or today is Thursday
    Today is not Wednesday
    So, today must be Thursday

4. Either you are rich or you are happy
    You are not happy
    So, you must be rich

5. You said it would be cold and it would rain
    But it isn't cold
    So, it won't rain

6. If we are in Glasgow then it must be raining
    It isn't raining
    So, we aren't in Glasgow

7. If you are healthy then you are happy
    You are not healthy
    So, you are not happy

8. If you don't drink milk then you won't have strong bones
    You do have strong bones
    So, you do drink milk

9. If you go to the casino then you may lose all your money
    If you lose all your money then you will be unable to pay the rent
    So, if you go to the casino then you will be unable to pay the rent

10. If you give me enough money then I can buy us a drink and something to eat
    I didn't buy us something to eat
    So, you didn't give me enough money

Answers

Answers to Exercise 5.1

1. *Any suitable example such as* Modus Ponens*: If P then Q. P, therefore Q.*

2. *The circles represent sets.*

3. *A shaded circle represents an empty set.*

4. *The 'x' symbol signifies that there is at least one member of that set (or some members of that set).*

5. *Whenever the conclusion of the argument can be read off from a diagram depicting only the premises.*

6. *'And' statements are only true when both halves of the conjunction are true (P and Q).*

7. *'If/then' statements are false only when P is true and Q is false.*

8. *The inclusive use of the words 'or' means 'one or other or both' while the exclusive use means 'one or other but not both.'*

9. *When every row containing all true premises also shows a true conclusion.*

10. *Venn diagrams and truth tables are limited in their usefulness because they can only deal with arguments of a limited complexity.*

Answers to Exercise 5.2

1. *Jack is happy*

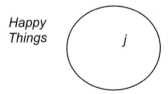

2. *The Prime Minister is not a Liberal Democrat*

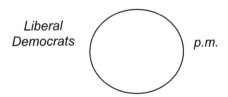

3. *Sarah is not perfect*

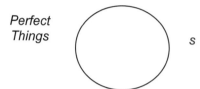

4. *Tehseen likes flowers*

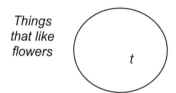

5. *Pedro hates Mondays*

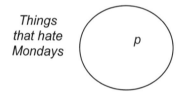

6. *All men are irritable*

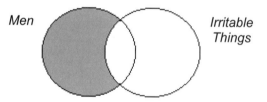

7. *Some restaurants are expensive*

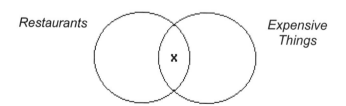

8. *No women are easily fooled*

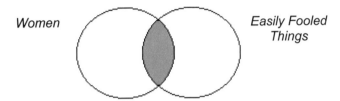

Women   Easily Fooled
                                                  Things

9. *Some dogs are not dangerous*

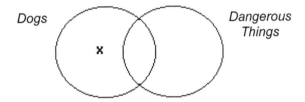

Dogs   Dangerous
                                               Things

10. *No soldiers are not well fed*

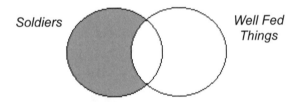

Soldiers   Well Fed
                                                  Things

Answers to Exercise 5.3

Test the validity of the following arguments using Venn diagrams:

1. *VALID*

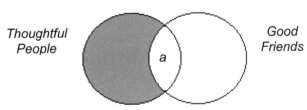

Thoughtful   Good
People   Friends

2. *VALID*

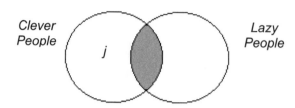

3. *VALID*

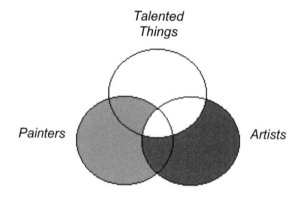

4. *INVALID*

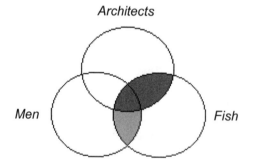

5. *INVALID*

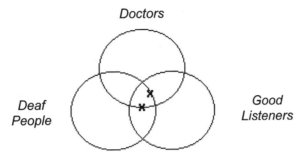

6. *VALID*

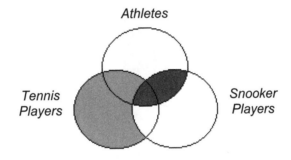

7. *VALID*

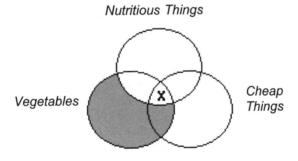

8. *INVALID*

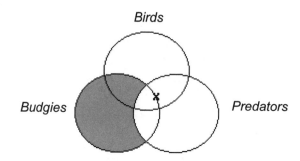

9. *INVALID*

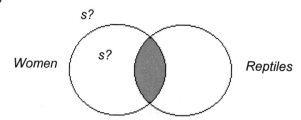

10. *INVALID*

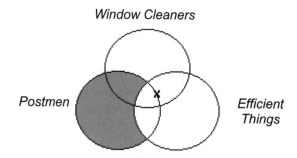

Answers to Exercise 5.4

1. *If you like music then you'll like Beethoven.*

P	Q	P → Q
T	T	T
T	F	F
F	T	T
F	F	T

2. *I am tired and I am hungry.*

P	Q	P & Q
T	T	T
T	F	F
F	T	F
F	F	F

3. *You're either a cat lover or you're a dog lover.*

P	Q	P v Q
T	T	T
T	F	T
F	T	T
F	F	F

4. *I am not rich.*

P	~ P
T	F
F	T

5. *'If we buy our ticket now we can go to the park and see the show.' This sentence has the form 'P → Q & R' which means it has three variables rather than two. This means it requires a larger truth table which allows for the eight possible truth combinations that three variables produce. When it comes to filling out the rest of the table we need to work out the values in three stages: first work out the values for P, then work out the values for Q & R and then use these two sets of values to work out the final values for P → Q & R'. These final values have been shown in bold.*

P	Q	R	P	→ Q & R	
T	T	T	T	**T**	T
T	T	F	T	**F**	F
T	F	T	T	**F**	F
T	F	F	T	**F**	F
F	T	T	F	**F**	T
F	T	F	F	**F**	F
F	F	T	F	**F**	F
F	F	F	F	**F**	F

6. *To be or not to be. This sentence has the form 'P v ~ P' and requires us to work out the values for 'P' and then '~ P' before we can work out the values for the whole statement 'P v ~ P'. These final values have been shown in bold.*

P	Q	P v ~ P
T	T	T **T** F
T	F	T **T** F
F	T	F **T** T
F	F	F **T** T

7. *You are not big or clever. This statement is tricky because it is negating the complex statement that 'you are big or clever.' It could be restated as 'It is not the case that (you are big or clever).' This means it has the form '~ (P v Q)' which requires us to work out the values inside the brackets before we can do the negation. These final values have been shown in bold.*

P	Q	~ (P v Q)
T	T	**F** T
T	F	**F** T
F	T	**F** T
F	F	**T** F

8. *Tehseen likes flowers.*

P	P
T	T
F	F

9. *Peter likes football and tennis.*

P	Q	P & Q
T	T	T
T	F	F
F	T	F
F	F	F

10. *You either like tea but don't like coffee or you don't like tea but do like coffee. This example involves working out the brackets before arriving at the final values. The final values have been shown in bold.*

P	Q	(P	&	~ Q)	v	(~ P	&	Q)
T	T	T	F	F	**F**	F	F	T
T	F	T	T	T	**T**	F	F	F
F	T	F	F	F	**F**	T	T	T
F	F	F	F	T	**F**	T	F	F

Answers to Exercise 5.5

1. *VALID. The first row proves validity.*

Variables		Premise 1	Premise 2	Conclusion
P	Q	P	Q	P & Q
T	T	T	T	T
T	F	T	F	F
F	T	F	T	F
F	F	F	F	F

2. *VALID. The first row proves validity.*

Variables		Premise 1	Premise 2	Conclusion
P	Q	P → Q	P	Q
T	T	T	T	T
T	F	F	T	F
F	T	T	F	T
F	F	T	F	F

3. *VALID. The third row proves validity.*

Variables		Premise 1	Premise 2	Conclusion
P	Q	P v Q	~ P	Q
T	T	T	F	T
T	F	T	F	F
F	T	T	T	T
F	F	F	T	F

113

4.　*VALID. The second row proves validity.*

Variables		Premise 1	Premise 2	Conclusion
P	**Q**	**P v Q**	**~ Q**	**P**
T	T	T	F	T
T	F	T	T	T
F	T	T	F	F
F	F	F	T	F

5.　*INVALID. This argument form never has all true premises.*

Variables		Premise 1	Premise 2	Conclusion
P	**Q**	**P & Q**	**~ P**	**~ Q**
T	T	T	F	F
T	F	F	F	T
F	T	F	T	F
F	F	F	T	T

6.　*VALID. The fourth row proves validity.*

Variables		Premise 1	Premise 2	Conclusion
P	**Q**	**P → Q**	**~ Q**	**~ P**
T	T	T	F	F
T	F	F	T	F
F	T	T	F	T
F	F	T	T	T

7.　*INVALID. The third row proves invalidity.*

Variables		Premise 1	Premise 2	Conclusion
P	**Q**	**P → Q**	**~ P**	**~ Q**
T	T	T	F	F
T	F	F	F	T
F	T	T	T	F
F	F	T	T	T

8. *VALID. The first row proves validity.*

Variables		Premise 1	Premise 2	Conclusion
P	**Q**	**~ P → ~ Q**	**Q**	**P**
T	T	T	T	T
T	F	T	F	T
F	T	F	T	F
F	F	T	F	F

9. *VALID. Every time all the premises are true, the conclusion is true. Rows 1, 5, 7 and 8 prove validity.*

Variables			Premise 1	Premise 2	Conclusion
P	**Q**	**R**	**P → Q**	**Q → R**	**P → R**
T	T	T	T	T	T
T	T	F	T	F	F
T	F	T	F	T	T
T	F	F	F	T	F
F	T	T	T	T	T
F	T	F	T	F	T
F	F	T	T	T	T
F	F	F	T	T	T

10. *VALID. Every time all the premises are true, the conclusion is true. Rows 6 and 8 prove validity.*

Variables			Premise 1	Premise 2	Conclusion
P	**Q**	**R**	**P → Q & R**	**~ R**	**~ P**
T	T	T	T	F	F
T	T	F	F	T	F
T	F	T	F	F	F
T	F	F	F	T	F
F	T	T	T	F	T
F	T	F	T	T	T
F	F	T	T	F	T
F	F	F	T	T	T

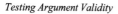

Chapter 6

Fallacies

What are Fallacies?

A **fallacy** is simply a flawed argument or an error in reasoning. Throughout this Book we have encountered numerous flawed arguments, but some mistakes in reasoning are so common that they can be categorised into groups and given special names (such as 'the fallacy of false dilemma' or 'the slippery slope fallacy'). By studying fallacies we can become aware of the most common types or error that people make when they try to construct an argument and so hopefully avoid making these same sorts of mistakes ourselves. However, this is not an easy task because the defining feature of fallacies is that they are all at first glance very convincing and it requires careful scrutiny to see exactly how they are leading us astray.

Fallacies are often divided into two main groups known as **formal fallacies** and **informal fallacies**. A formal fallacy is an argument that usually has an invalid structure, while an informal fallacy can be structurally valid, but relies on false premises or some other non-rational means to convince the opponent.

Formal Fallacies

Formal fallacies are identified by looking at their structure alone. It's not the content of the argument that is at fault here, but simply they way the argument has been put together. Formal fallacies are therefore usually invalid although there are some notable exceptions, such as **circular arguments**, which are technically valid but have a structure which always fails to convince.

Two of the most common formal fallacies are **denying the antecedent** and **affirming the consequent**.

Denying the Antecedent

Denying the antecedent is the name given to any argument with the structure:

- If P then Q
  Not P
  Not Q

For example:

- If you are Scottish then you are British
  You are not Scottish
  So, you can't be British

At first this might look appealing, but on closer inspection this argument is invalid. We can't infer that someone isn't British just because they aren't Scottish. After all, English, Welsh and Northern Irish people are British and they aren't Scottish. This fallacy arises because it is easy to confuse the statement 'If you are Scottish then you are British' with the statement '*Only* if you are Scottish then you are British.' Had the argument used this latter premise it would have been valid.

Affirming the Consequent

Affirming the consequent looks very similar to denying the antecedent, but is subtly different. This is when an argument has the form:

- If P then Q
  Q
  P

Such as:

- If you are Scottish then you are British
  You are British
  So, you must be Scottish

This is also invalid. Just because all Scottish people are British we can't assume all British people are Scottish (again, English, Welsh and Northern Irish people are British but not Scottish).

What makes denying the antecedent and affirming the consequent initially appealing is that they have a superficial similarity with two very common valid argument forms, known as **affirming the antecedent** (also known as *modus ponens*) and **denying the consequent** (also known as *modus tollens*).

Affirming the antecedent is possibly one of the most common valid argument forms and looks like this:

- If P then Q
  <u>P</u>
  Q

- If you are Scottish then you are British
  You are Scottish
  So, you must be British

This is clearly valid because if both the premises are true then the conclusion must be true.

Denying the consequent is a more surprising valid form because, intuitively, it looks invalid, but is in fact perfectly well structured.

- If P then Q
  <u>Not Q</u>
  Not P

- If you are Scottish then you are British
  You are not British
  So, you can't be Scottish

This might seem like unreliable reasoning, but if we accept that all Scottish people are British, then anyone who isn't British will be automatically excluded from being Scottish (they can't be English, Welsh or Northern Irish either).

Circular Reasoning

A circular argument is one in where the premises assume the truth of the conclusion. In fact, in some simple circular arguments the premise simply *is* the conclusion. Such arguments would have the form:

- <u>P</u>
  P

An example might be:

- 'My dad is better than your dad because he's the best Dad out of them both.'

This is a circular argument because the premise 'My dad's the best dad out of them both' assumes that the conclusion 'My dad is better than your dad', is true. However, circular arguments can have more complex and sophisticated appearances than this one. This fallacy is also sometimes known as the fallacy of **begging the question** and has the Latin name ***petitio principii***.

The curious thing about the fallacy of circular reasoning is that circular arguments are capable of being both valid and sound. Consider the following example:

- The earth is round
  Therefore, the earth is round

This argument is valid because the conclusion will always follow from the premise in virtue of the fact that the premise *is* the conclusion in this case. Moreover, since the premise also happens to be true, the argument now satisfies all our conditions of a sound argument: true premises plus a valid structure. So, why is this type of argument deemed fallacious?

Circular arguments are usually regarded as fallacies because they fail to achieve the primary goal of any argument: to convince others. Arguments try to move people from premises they do accept towards conclusions that they initially did not. However, where the premise requires the acceptance of the conclusion there would be no argument in the first place. Anyone who didn't accept the conclusion wouldn't accept the premise either. Circular arguments are therefore necessarily unconvincing.

Informal Fallacies

Informal fallacies are not identified by their structure, but by their use of non-rational means to win the argument. For example, an informal fallacy might use misleading premises; make questionable assumptions or rely on the use of emotive language to convince you that the conclusion is true. Informal fallacies are therefore capable of being perfectly valid, but they are almost always unsound because of their reliance on dubious premises.

False Dilemma

The term **false dilemma** refers to arguments which try to convince their opponent that there are only two options available, when in fact there may be a number of options available. They often have the valid form:

- P or Q
  $\underline{P}$
  Q

For example:

- 'Either you support Celtic Football Club or you support Rangers Football Club, and since you don't support Celtic you must be a Rangers supporter.'

This argument is unsound because the first premise is false. It is not the case that all people either support Celtic or Rangers. There are people who support Partick Thistle or Manchester United. Hence, the dilemma which the opponent is being faced with is a false one. There are some situations, though, which are genuine dilemmas and arguments based on these are not fallacious. For example:

- 'Either you will win the lottery or you will not win the lottery. If you win the lottery your riches will destroy your happiness, as wealth always does. But, if you do not win the lottery you will remain penniless and continue to endure the miseries of poverty.'

This isn't obviously a false dilemma at all since there are genuinely only two possibilities in this case – either you will win the lottery or you will not (although you may wish to disagree with the consequences that allegedly ensue from these two possibilities).

Argument from Ignorance

An **argument from ignorance** actually describes two related types of argument. One version makes the mistake of assuming that something is true because it has not been proven false, and the other wrongly assumes that something is false because it has not been proven true. In Latin the argument from ignorance is known as the ***argumentum ad ignorantiam***. Examples might include:

- 'Einstein believed that black holes must exist. However, a black hole has never actually been observed anywhere in the universe so Einstein was wrong.'

- 'Believing in supernatural spirits isn't as odd as you might think. No one has ever demonstrated that the spirits of the dead don't exist so it makes perfect sense to believe that they do.'

The fallacy of arguing from ignorance arises because while we should demand proof for the statements we believe it is extremely difficult, if not impossible, to prove a negative. While we could easily demonstrate that the Loch Ness monster exists, by say, catching it in a fishing net, what would the evidence look like for its non-existence? There is a joke which centres on this very point:

- Question: What is white, yellow and invisible?
  Answer: No eggs.

In they same way that it is absurd to talk descriptively about 'no eggs', how could we show someone 'no monster'?

Illegitimate Appeals to Authority

An **appeal to authority** is an argument that cites some eminent source in order to support the conclusion of the argument. This is of course something we do all the time on matters where expert opinion is needed, such as theoretical physics or the life and times of Alexander the Great. However, it is often seen as a weaker form of arguing than giving independent reasons for something. Appeals to authority are sometimes given the Latin name *argumentum ad verecundiam* or *argumentum ad auctoritatem* and can be unreliable for a number of reasons. Consider the following examples:

1. I read a book once which says that there is no highest prime number.
2. Oscar winning actor Denzel Washington says that there is no highest prime number.
3. Professor Jones, the professor of mathematics at Harvard University says that there is no highest prime number.

The first example backs up a claim by appealing to a book in which this claim was contained. However, this is a case of appealing to an unnamed authority and normally we require the source of the claim to be identified before we accept it. The second examples cites an authority who, while distinguished and eminent, is not a leading expert in the field in question, so is therefore an illegitimate authority to appeal to. The third example is better because the authority cited *is* a leading expert in the relevant field. We might say therefore that it creates a stronger argument than the other two.

However, even this last example is open to criticism in the eyes of some logicians. This is because they would argue that although it is true that there is no highest prime number, it is not true *because* Professor Jones says it. Its truth is based on reasons independent of the person who makes the claim. Therefore, some people would take the view that *any* appeal to authority is unjustified. However, this might seem a rather extreme stance to take since we do make use of appeals to authority in everyday life, and most modern day logicians would accept that an appeal to a relevant expert might provide strong reasons to believe a particular claim. This is why this fallacy is now specifically referred to as the ***illegitimate* appeal to authority**.

Slippery Slope

Slippery slope fallacies work by assuming that a premise leads inevitably to a conclusion without providing conclusive proof that it does. Usually, these arguments use numerous premises to arrive at the conclusion through a series of small, incremental steps. This forms a 'slippery slope' because once you have accepted the first premise you have already granted everything.

- 'If we ban religion in schools, then it won't be long before we ban philosophy and history too. If we ban philosophy and history we will soon have a state controlled curriculum. Once we have a state controlled curriculum we will no longer be freethinking citizens. A society without freethinking citizens is a totalitarian state. So, we must defend the teaching of religion at all costs.'

This argument is a good example of the slippery slope at work and such arguments can be fallacious for a number of different reasons. Sometimes the most controversial premise is the opening one, so after accepting this premise it becomes impossible to avoid the conclusion. On these occasions the opening premise is false and so the argument is simply unsound. In other examples each step in the slope alleges a causal connection which may be very tenuous indeed, therefore the more steps the argument has the less reliable it becomes. This is why this argument is sometimes referred to in Latin as a type on ***non causa pro causa*** argument which means that the argument postulates a 'non-cause for a cause.'

Slippery slope arguments often have a form like this:

- If P then Q
  If Q then R
  If R then S
  If P then S

However, it is not the case that any argument which makes use of a slippery slope approach is a fallacy. If each link in the argument chain is well supported then such an argument could be both valid and sound. For example:

- If you are a woman then you are a human
  If you are a human then you are a mammal
  If you are a mammal then you are a vertebrate
  If you are a vertebrate then you can't be jellyfish
  So, if you are a woman, you can't be a jellyfish

Coincidental Correlation

The **coincidental correlation** argument is also known in Latin as the ***post hoc ergo propter hoc*** fallacy (which is a bit of a mouthful). This is when an argument wrongly assumes that because one event is always seen to precede another that it must therefore be the cause of the other. The Latin term *post hoc ergo propter hoc* means 'after this therefore *because* of this.' This is a fallacy because we cannot assume that all things which are correlated must be causally related. To say that two things are 'correlated' simply means that they are found to occur together, but to say they are 'causally liked' is to make the stronger claim that there is some sort of necessary connection between them. Some examples of post hoc fallacies are clearly cases of misguided reasoning:

- 'The cockerel crows before the sun comes up every day, so the cockerel must cause the sun to come up.'

Other examples, though, are less obviously misguided and might require further investigation before we can be certain how erroneous they are. For example:

- 'After the death penalty was abolished in Britain the number of murders increased. So, the death penalty must be reintroduced to help cut the number of murders.'

While the facts in the above example are true, the abolition of the death penalty in Britain in the 1960's also coincided with significant social changes, which may have also impacted on the crime rate. So, again we may not be justified in assuming that one caused the other.

Even with more clear-cut examples, we must still be vigilant for post hoc reasoning:

- 'After I pressed the switch the light went on, so the switch must have caused the light to go on.'

This might seem reasonable enough given our past experience of lights and switches. However, strictly speaking, this could be seen as fallacious too. Even if it is true that the switch really has caused the light to go on, it might still be fallacious to argue that we can infer this conclusion from the correlation of the two events *alone*. We could therefore conclude that this post hoc fallacy is, strictly speaking, invalid since it is possible for the premise to be true while the conclusion is false.

Because coincidental correlation allege a false cause to an event they are sometimes classified as a type of *non causa pro causa* fallacy, along with slippery slope arguments.

Attacking the Person

An argument is guilty of **attacking the person** when it focuses on the character of their opponent rather than the statement that their opponent supports. Arguments like this are seen in courtrooms everyday:

- 'How can you believe the testimony of that witness? He's an unemployed layabout who has never done an honest day's work in his life!'

Of course, this line of argument is fallacious because the character of the opponent may be entirely irrelevant to the truth or falsity of the statements they support.

It is perfectly possible to construct a valid argument that attacks the person. One could do so along the following lines:

- If the witness is a layabout then his testimony is worthless
  The witness is a layabout
  Therefore, his testimony is worthless

However, even if we charitably reconstructed the argument as above, it would still fail to be a *sound* argument because it is not obvious that the opening premise is true. A layabout can still give an accurate testimony.

In Latin, the attacking the person fallacy is known as the ***argumentum ad hominem*** and you might see it described as such in other textbooks (*ad hominem* means 'against the man'). However, there are actually three distinct types of *ad hominem* argument known as ***ad hominem abusive***, ***ad hominem circumstantial*** and ***ad hominem tu quoque***.

Ad Hominem Abusive

The ad hominem abusive variation is probably the most common version of attacking the person. Here the argument simply throws mud on the character of their opponent as we demonstrated in the argument above. Another example could be:

- 'How can you support the policies of the Liberal Democrats? Their leader is a numpty!'

Again, a policy could still be a correct one even if championed by a so-called 'numpty'.

Ad Hominem Circumstantial

Ad hominem circumstantial occurs when someone questions the relationship between the circumstances of their opponent and the statements they support. For example:

- 'You voted Conservative because you claim that they are the best party for government. However, you're only voting for them because they've promised tax cuts for people your age! The conservatives are therefore not the best party for government.'

This argument is fallacious because rather than trying to provide reasons to support the view that the Conservatives are not the best party for government, the argument instead insinuates a corrupt connection between the claim and the circumstances of the opponent. However, whether I personally benefit from supporting a statement or not is irrelevant to the issue of whether that statement is true or not.

Ad Hominem Tu Quoque

Ad hominem tu quoque is the term used to describe arguments which allege that someone doesn't practise what they preach (*tu quoque* is Latin for 'you too'). However, just because someone's actions do not concur with the statements they support, we cannot conclude that their statements are therefore false. An example might be:

- 'Rock stars always tell us to stay away from drugs, but most of them have been drug addicts all their lives!'

Appeal to Consequences

An appeal to consequences is where someone alleges that a statement must be false simply because accepting the statement might have undesirable results. Clearly, the fact that a proposition has undesirable consequences is irrelevant to the issue of whether that proposition is true or not. It is known in Latin as ***argumentum ad consequentiam***. An example might be:

- 'It can't be the case that joining the Euro currency is the right thing for Britain. If we did we would lose the pound and everyone would have to convert their money.'

This argument is an example of the appeal to consequences fallacy, because joining the Euro could still be the right thing to do despite this particular negative consequence. However, we mustn't assume that any argument which contains a reference to consequences must be fallacious. In situations when the consequences of a belief have a bearing on its truth or falsity, we might be entitled to make such an appeal.

- 'If we don't get a job we won't have any money this week. Neither of us wants to be left without any money this week, so we'd better get a job.'

This might look like an appeal to consequences fallacy, but in this case the consequence *is* relevant to the truth of the claim that they must get a job. Another example of a legitimate appeal to consequences might be:

- 'Ban boxing now because it causes cumulative brain damage to boxers.'

Again, the negative consequences of boxing are in this case very relevant to the issue of whether we should ban boxing or not.

Chapter Summary

- ✓ A fallacy is an error in reasoning that occurs in an argument.

- ✓ Fallacies can arise for a number of very different reasons.

- ✓ Some fallacies are so common that they are often given special names.

- ✓ Fallacies are sometimes divided in formal and informal types.

- ✓ A formal fallacy is an argument that has an invalid structure such as 'denying the antecedent.'

- ✓ An informal fallacy is one which can be structurally valid, but may make use of a false or irrelevant premise such as 'false dilemma.'

- ✓ Circular arguments, while fallacious, can be both technically valid and sound.

- ✓ Some arguments have the structure or appearance of fallacies, but can be perfectly sound arguments on closer consideration.

Exercises

Answers to the following exercises can be found at the end of this chapter. If you have any difficulties with any of these questions refer back to the text of Chapter 6.

Exercise 6.1

Answer the following questions in your own words:

1. What is a fallacy?

2. Are all fallacies invalid? Explain your answer.

3. Are all fallacies unsound? Explain your answer.

4. What is the difference between a formal fallacy and an informal fallacy?

5. What is the form of arguments guilty of 'denying the antecedent'?

6. Are all dilemmas false dilemmas?

7. What is the difference between illegitimate appeals to authority and legitimate appeals to authority?

8. What makes 'slippery slope' arguments slippery?

9. Give your own example of two events which are often correlated, but have no causal connection between them.

10. What differentiates the *'tu quoque'* version of the 'attacking the person' fallacy from other versions?

Exercise 6.2

Explain the following fallacies in your own words:

1. Denying the antecedent.

2. Affirming the consequent.

3. Circular reasoning.

4. False dilemma.

5. Arguing from ignorance.

6. Slippery slope.

7. Attacking the person.

8. Appeal to authority.

9. Appeal to consequences.

10. Coincidental correlation.

Exercise 6.3

Provide the more conventional names for the following types of argument:

1. *Argumentum ad hominem.*

2. *Argumentum ad verecundiam.*

3. *Argumentum ad consequentiam.*

4. *Post hoc ergo propter hoc.*

5. *Modus tollens.*

6. *Modus ponens.*

7. *Petitio principii.*

8. *Argumentum ad auctoritatem.*

9. *Argumentum ad ignorantiam.*

10. *Non causa pro causa.*

Exercise 6.4

Identify which fallacies are being committed in the following arguments:

1. Quantum physics must be nonsense. If it were true then the very existence of matter would be down to mere chance.

2. Whenever I see Bill, Peter is never around. Yet as soon as I catch up with Peter, Bill is nowhere to be seen. I'm beginning to suspect that Peter and Bill are the same person!

3. The trouble with Scotland is that you've either got to love it or leave it.

4. If you don't get a plaster for that cut then your finger could get infected and if it does it could get gangrenous. If that happens you could lose a hand or even a whole limb or worse still your infection will spread to others and wipe out the entire family or even the whole town.

5. How can you agree with the Conservative's policy on education? Most of them went to private school and don't have a clue about state education.

6.   The developing nations must have all their debt removed. Bono from U2 says this is the only way that they can even begin to address poverty.

7.   As far as the environment goes, either you are part of the problem or you are part of the solution and since you don't recycle you must be part of the problem.

8.   Everyone knows that if you lie out in the sun too long you'll get sunburn. You must have been lying in the sun too long because you have the worst case of sunburn I've ever seen.

9.   Fox hunting is wrong because it's just plain immoral to hunt foxes.

10. Despite the scare stories in the press, child vaccinations are harmless and help protect against serious illnesses. Medical research has consistently failed to show any conclusive link between autism and vaccination in childhood.

Exercise 6.5

Some of the following arguments contain fallacies and some do not. If they contain a fallacy state the name of the fallacy. If they do not commit a fallacy explain why not.

1.   Either you are pregnant or you are not. If you are you'll need a pre-natal check and if you aren't you'll need to find out why you feel sick each morning. Either way, you'll need to go to the doctor.

2.   Everyone knows that if you stand out in the rain you'll catch a cold. You have a cold so you must have been standing in the rain.

3.   I had the laser eye surgery and my eyesight improved. The laser surgery must have improved my eyesight.

4.   If we allow euthanasia with the patient's consent then it won't be long before we allow it without their consent. Soon we'll be killing the old and frail and eventually we'll be killing children too. Eventually we'll be wiping out the whole human race. Therefore, we shouldn't legalise euthanasia.

5.   If you don't pay me back my money I'll send the boys round to beat you up. You don't want that to happen so you'd better pay me now.

6.   If you eat your vegetables you'll grow up healthy. You never eat your vegetables so you won't grow up healthy.

7.   If you keep refusing to eat anything you'll get weaker and weaker. Eventually you won't be able to go to work and ultimately you will die. Therefore, you should eat something soon.

8. Mother Theresa said that having a family was the best way to live your life. However, she was a nun and didn't have any children of her own so we can't give her views much weight.

9. The Chairman of the Bank of England predicts interest rates will go up next month, so you'd better buy your house now before it gets more expensive.

10. You either live on your own or you stay at home with your parents. Since you can't afford to live on your own, you'll have to stay with your parents.

Answers

Answers to Exercise 6.1

1. *A fallacy is a mistake in reasoning contained in an argument.*

2. *Not all fallacies are invalid. Some fallacies can be well structured but use false premises.*

3. *Not all fallacies are unsound. Circular arguments can be both valid and sound. They are just unconvincing.*

4. *A formal fallacy is an argument with an invalid structure. An informal fallacy is an argument which is valid but makes use of false or irrelevant premises.*

5. *If P then Q. Not P. Therefore Not Q.*

6. *Not all dilemmas are false dilemmas. In situations where there are only two options the dilemma is a genuine one.*

7. *Illegitimate appeals to authority make use of irrelevant sources to support a claim such as people who are not an expert in the relevant field. Legitimate appeals to authority cite an appropriate source.*

8. *Slippery slope arguments contain a number of small steps which lead to an inexorable slide towards the conclusion. Often, once you have granted the opening premise you have granted everything.*

9. *Any suitable example will do. For example, every time I watch the San Marino national football team they lose, therefore if I didn't watch them they would win.*

10. *The 'tu quoque' version of attacking the person alleges that the opponent does not practice what they preach.*

Answers to Exercise 6.2

1. *Denying the antecedent: A formal fallacy which occurs when arguments have the invalid form 'If P then Q. Not P, therefore Q'.*

2. *Affirming the consequent: A formal fallacy which occurs when arguments have the invalid form 'If P then Q. Q, therefore P'.*

3. *Circular reasoning: An argument which assumes the truth of the conclusion in one of its premises.*

4. *False dilemma: An argument which wrongly claims that there are only two*

options in a situation when there may be more.

5. *Arguing from ignorance: An argument which assumes that lack of proof for something can be taken as evidence that it must therefore be false.*

6. *Slippery slope: An argument which arrives at a false conclusion by a series of incremental steps, some of which may be false.*

7. *Attacking the person: An argument that attacks the character of the opponent as a way of demonstrating that what they believe must therefore be false.*

8. *Appeal to authority: An argument which asserts that something is true by pointing to some eminent source for the claim.*

9. *Appeal to consequences: An argument which claims that a statement must be false simply because of the negative consequences which might ensue from supporting it.*

10. *Coincidental correlation: An argument which wrongly assumes that two correlated events must have a causal relationship between them.*

Answers to Exercise 6.3

1. Argumentum ad hominem*: Attacking the person.*

2. Argumentum ad verecundiam*: Appeal to authority.*

3. Argumentum ad consequentiam*: Appeal to consequences.*

4. Post hoc ergo propter hoc*: Coincidental correlation.*

5. Modus tollens*: Denying the consequent (which is not a fallacy).*

6. Modus ponens*: Affirming the antecedent (which is not a fallacy).*

7. Petitio principii*: Circular reasoning or begging the question.*

8. Argumentum ad auctoritatem*: Another name for appeal to authority.*

9. Argumentum ad ignorantiam*: Argument from ignorance.*

10. Non causa pro causa*: Could refer to slippery slope or coincidental correlation arguments.*

Answers to Exercise 6.4

1. *Appeal to consequences.*

2. *Coincidental correlation.*

3. *False dilemma.*

4. *Slippery slope.*

5. *Attacking the person.*

6. *Appeal to authority.*

7. *False dilemma.*

8. *Affirming the consequent.*

9. *Circular reasoning.*

10. *Arguing from ignorance.*

Answers to Exercise 6.5

1. *Not a fallacy. This looks like false dilemma but the opening premise is true: you are either pregnant or you are not. You can't be a little bit pregnant so the dilemma is a genuine one.*

2. *This is a case of the affirming the consequent fallacy.*

3. *Not a fallacy. The correlation of events here is presumably not coincidental.*

4. *This is a slippery slope fallacy.*

5. *Not a fallacy. This looks like an appeal to consequences fallacy, but in this case the consequences are pertinent to the truth of the conclusion.*

6. *This is a case of the denying the antecedent fallacy.*

7. *Not a fallacy. This looks like a slippery slope fallacy, but in this case each step in the argument is true.*

8. *This is an example of the attacking the person fallacy (the* tu quoque *variation). Mother Theresa's views could still be true even if she doesn't practice what she preaches.*

9. *Not a fallacy. This looks like an example of an illegitimate appeal to authority, but in this case the authority is a legitimate one.*

10. *This is a false dilemma because there are more than two options available: you could share a flat with someone else or go live with your aunt.*

Chapter 7
Study and Revision Guide

Preparing for Assessment

This chapter offers some advice and some study tools which may be of use to those who are preparing for assessments for the Higher or Intermediate 2 units in Critical Thinking offered by the SQA. However, these materials could benefit anyone preparing for exams offered by other examining bodies.

The key activities you should be engaged in when you have a forthcoming test are:

- Clarifying the mandatory content of the course or unit you are studying (you cannot be asked a question that is out with the course or unit content).
- Making up study sheets for each topic to help you revise.
- Practicing your skills by doing past papers and practice questions.
- Sorting out any remaining areas of confusion by referring to books and web resources.

Each of these activities is addressed below.

SQA Unit Requirements

In preparing for internal or external assessments your starting point should be clarifying precisely what the unit requirements are for your relevant level of study. The SQA assessment strategy for these units makes use of sampling, which means that you will not necessarily be assessed on every part of the unit, but you have no way of knowing which components will be assessed.

Intermediate 2 Critical Thinking

The central skills required by the Intermediate 2 unit in Critical Thinking are:

- Explain the purpose of arguments.
- Distinguish between statements and arguments.

- Understand the structure of arguments in terms of premises and conclusions.
- Distinguish reliable from unreliable arguments.
- Be able to identify a range of common unreliable arguments, namely:
  o Attacking the person
  o Appeals to consequences
  o Illegitimate appeals to authority
  o Argument from ignorance.

Internal assessments and external assessments at Intermediate 2 level are marked out of 10. In internal assessments the mark allocation is divided 70:30 with 70% of marks awarded for *knowledge and understanding* (e.g. defining key terms), and 30% of marks awarded for *analysis and evaluation* (e.g. assessing the reliability of an unseen argument). In external assessments (the end of year SQA exams) this ratio changes to a more demanding 60:40 ratio, with 60% of marks being awarded for knowledge and understanding and 40% for analysis and evaluation. The marks for knowledge and understanding and analysis and evaluation are clearly marked *'KU'* and *'AE'*, respectively, on the exam paper.

Higher Critical Thinking

The central skills required by the Higher unit in Critical Thinking are:

- Explain the purpose of arguments.
- Distinguish between statements and arguments.
- Understand the structure of arguments in terms of premises and conclusions.
- Identify hidden premises.
- Identify valid and sound arguments.
- Distinguish deductive reasoning from inductive reasoning.
- Identify a range of common unreliable arguments, namely:
  o Attacking the person
  o Appeals to consequences
  o Illegitimate appeals to authority
  o Argument from ignorance
  o Circular reasoning
  o Slippery slope
  o *Post hoc ergo propter hoc*
  o False dilemma.

Internal assessments and external assessments at Higher level are marked out of 20 because of the additional content. In internal assessments the mark allocation is divided 60:40 with 60% of marks awarded for *knowledge and understanding* and 40% of marks awarded for *analysis and evaluation*. In external assessments (the end of year SQA exams) marks are split evenly with 50% of marks being awarded for knowledge and understanding and 50% for analysis and evaluation. As with Intermediate 2, the marks for knowledge and understanding and analysis and evaluation are clearly marked *KU* and *AE*, respectively, on the exam paper.

How to Create a Study Sheet

Study sheets are an excellent way of organising your knowledge in preparation for a closed book examination situation. A good study sheet effectively summarises everything you know on a topic into one or two pages of A4 paper. Study sheets work because they organise the information into a meaningful order; they force you to revise everything you need to know and they are an active rather than passive way of studying. Reading a book is a passive way of studying because you are seeing the information organised for you by someone else. A study sheet more actively engages you by allowing you to decide which way to organise the material, so making you much more likely to remember it.

They key components of a good study sheet are:

- It should be short.
- It should be neat and easy to read.
- It should contain trigger words rather than a lot of long sentences.
- It should try to break up the conventional linear order of your notes.
- It should group similar things together using boxes.
- It should use arrows to show connections between things.
- It might use different colours of ink (too many will make it confusing though).
- It could include pictures.
- It could include mnemonics and other memory aids.
- It should be the best of a number of drafts, each version being better organised, neater and more succinct than the last.

Once you have finished a study sheet you will find that you don't really need it because it is the process of creating it that has made the knowledge stick in your head. One hour spent making up a good study sheet is better than three hours reading a book. Study sheets should also be the last thing you look at before you enter an exam. If you see someone leafing through an enormous folder of notes before an exam you are probably looking at someone about to fail.

An example of a study sheet for the fallacies topic is given below:

Logical Fallacies

What is a Fallacy?

- A fallacy is a faulty argument

- Fallacies can be faulty for a number of different reasons

- Fallacies can be categorised as formal fallacies or informal fallacies:

  o A **Formal Fallacy** is an argument with an invalid form

  o An **Informal Fallacy** might be formally valid but often has a dubious premise, so rendering it unsound

- Some fallacies, like Circular Arguments, can be both valid and sound!

4. Attacking the Person

- Arguments that attack the person who is presenting a point of view rather than the viewpoint they support

- If Peter is a drunk then we can disregard his views on drinking
  Peter is a drunk
  Therefore, we can disregard his views on drinking

- Also known as *Argument ad Hominem*

- Comes in three versions:

  ❖ *Ad Hominem Abusive*: Where a personal slur is made on the arguer

  ❖ *Ad Hominem Circumstantial*: Where it is alleged that the arguer profits from their adopted position

  ❖ *Ad Hominem Tu Quoque*: Where it is alleged that the arguer doesn't practice what they preach

Some Informal Fallacies

1. **False Dilemma**
- Arguments that make out there are only 2 options when there may be more

- You must either support *Celtic* or *Rangers*
  You don't support *Celtic*
  So, you must support *Rangers*

2. **Arguing from Ignorance**
- Arguments that assume that lack of proof of a proposition is proof of the contrary

- If there is no evidence of the Loch Ness monster then it doesn't exist. There is No evidence. So, it doesn't exist

3. **Slippery Slope**
- Arguments which make increasingly unlikely claims to arrive at a radical conclusion from seemingly innocuous premises

- If you ban guns you ban all weapons
  If you ban all weapons you ban all liberties
  If you ban all liberties then freedom is lost
  So, if you ban guns then freedom is lost

- If P then Q
  If Q then R
  If R then S
  If P then S

Fallacies that Make an Appeal

5. **Illegitimate Appeals to Consequences**
- Arguments that reject a proposition just because of its unfavourable or unsavoury consequences

- If evolution is right then we're all just monkeys. We can't be all mere monkeys. So, evolution can't be right

6. **Illegitimate Appeals to Authority**
- Arguments that try to support a proposition by pointing to some eminent source

- If Descartes said *God exists* then He must
  Descartes did say *God exists*
  So, *God* must exist

Fallacies
(Continued)

More Informal Fallacies

7.   Coincidental Correlation
- Arguments that assume that just because one event *follows* another, that the first event must have *caused* the other

- If cancer rates increase then the nuclear plant is dangerous
  Cancer rates have increased
  So, the nuclear plant must be dangerous

- If P then Q
  P
  Q

8.   Circular Reasoning
- Arguments where the truth of the conclusion is presumed by the premises. In other words these are Circular Arguments

- Aberdeen are a great football team
  Therefore, Aberdeen are a great football team

- P
  P

Two Formal Fallacies

9.   Denying the Antecedent

- Any argument with the underlying invalid form

- If P then Q
  Not P
  Not Q

- If you are Scottish then you are British
  You are not Scottish
  So, you are not British

10. Affirming the Consequent

- Any argument with the underlying invalid form

- If P then Q
  Q
  P

- If you are Scottish then you are British

Arguments that look like Fallacies but aren't

- Affirming the Antecedent (*Modus Ponens*)

- Any argument with the valid form:

If P then Q	If you are Scottish then you are British
P	You are Scottish
Q	So, you must be British

- Denying the Consequent (*Modus Tollens*)

- Any argument with the valid form:

If P then Q	If you are Scottish then you are British
Not Q	You are not British
Not P	So, you are not Scottish

Summary

1.   Denying the Antecedent
2.   Affirming the Consequent
3.   False Dilemma
4.   Arguing from Ignorance
5.   Slippery Slope
6.   Attacking the Person
7.   Appeal to Authority
8.   Appeal to Consequences
9.   Coincidental Correlation
10. Circular Reasoning

Some Common Concerns Answered

Many people struggle with critical thinking and logic courses and feel they are the only ones who don't 'get it' and are frightened by impending exams. However, it is important not to become dejected as almost all students of the subject have the same worries and concerns. The most common questions that students ask are addressed below:

1. Other people in my class seem to be picking this up quicker than me. Am I stupid?

No you are not. Like Maths, Critical Thinking is a subject that some people are annoyingly good at, while others need more effort. This is because everyone's brain works differently. Some psychologists explain these differences with reference to the different functions of the right and left hemispheres of the brain. People with a dominant left hemisphere are good at logical thinking and do well in linear tasks and number crunching. People with a dominant right side are often good at creative tasks such as art and are sometimes gifted communicators with a knack for languages. Left-brained people are good at deduction and usually pick up critical thinking easily, while right-brained people are sometimes good at seeing unusual solutions to problems and are able to 'think outside the box.' The important thing to realise is that we are all capable of using both sides of our brains with practice.

2. Do I need to memorise the Latin names for all the fallacies?

No, but you probably will. Examiners don't mind which names you use as long as you identify the fallacy correctly. Strangely enough though, the more unusual something is the more likely you are to remember it. Because we don't encounter Latin words that often they appear as novelties and so stick with us. Most students of critical thinking actually enjoy using the Latin names possibly because it makes them sound clever and allows them to show off to their friends.

3. I'm terrible at truth tables and Venn diagrams. Do I need to know them for the exam?

No. You do not need to know them for the SQA Critical Thinking units and cannot be asked to produce one. However, you can master anything with practice.

4. If I won't be assessed on Venn diagrams and truth tables why should I bother with them?

While Venn diagrams and truth tables are not part of the examined content of SQA courses they are still extremely handy to know. If you don't know how to do Venn diagrams or truth tables then you have very few tools at your disposal for checking the validity of an argument. While you may not be explicitly asked to create a Venn diagram you could still be required to say whether an argument is valid or not. Some arguments are obviously invalid, but others are not so obvious and it is on these occasions that it is useful to check your guess with a diagram. A mastery of Venn diagrams and truth tables will also prepare you for more advanced levels of study in this area.

5. The more books I read about critical thinking and logic the more confused I get.

This is because some books on critical thinking and logic go *way* beyond what you need for an introductory course. Such books are aimed at university level study and include advanced areas of logic. Steer clear of these texts when you are starting out. Another problem with referring to other texts is that different logicians use different definitions and different systems of notation from one another. This isn't because they are wrong but because they want their system of logic to do different things and cope with a larger range of arguments than we are dealing with in this Book. Furthermore, unlike maths, there really isn't any internationally agreed system of notation for logic. Some logicians invent their own symbols whilst others use familiar symbols in unfamiliar ways. So, unusually, critical thinking is a subject where it is actually advisable to not read too many books, at least at first: otherwise you will get confused between contradictory definitions and symbols.

Useful Websites

- **Philosophy Pages** (www.philosophypages.com)

  This is a very useful site by Garth Kemerling for students of philosophy in general, but also for students of logic and critical thinking in particular. The site contains an excellent dictionary of philosophical terms which explains technical terms clearly. There is also an elementary logic section which explains the basics very well. Beware of the section on logical symbols, though, as it uses different notation from the symbols used in this Book. (Remember, there is no set standard of notation for logical symbols; there are several accepted systems.)

- **Fallacy Files** (www.fallacyfiles.org)

  Easily the best internet website on fallacies. It is truly comprehensive and rigorously documents and exemplifies hundreds of known fallacies.

- **SQA Support Notes** (www.ltscotland.org.uk)

  The official support materials for SQA critical thinking courses, produced by the Scottish Further Education Unit (SFEU), can be downloaded free of charge from the Learning and Teaching Scotland (LTS) website. To locate them simply type 'critical thinking' into the search engine on the LTS website homepage.

Further Reading

Again, given the variety of accepted systems of notation in the world of critical thinking and logic, it is not recommended that you explore too many sources at first. However, some good basic introductions are:

- Mary Haight *The Snake and the Fox* (Routledge, 1999)

- John Nolt and Dennis Rohatyn et al *Schaum's Outlines: Logic* (McGraw Hill, 1988)

- Harry Gensler *An Introduction to Logic* (Routledge, 2001)

Practice Assessments

This section contains two practice assessments: one for the SQA Intermediate 2 unit and one for the SQA Higher unit. You may wish to use them to test your performance under timed conditions. The layout and mark allocations exactly mirror the layout of the current SQA external exams. Answers are provided at the end of this chapter.

Intermediate 2 Critical Thinking Practice Assessment

1. Read the following argument then answer the questions that follow.

"God must exist because belief in God promotes respect for others. If people didn't believe in God then society would be in a terrible state."

---

a) What is an argument? (*1 KU*)

b) What is the difference between a statement and an argument? (*2 KU*)

c) What are the premises of the above argument? (*2 KU*)

d) What is the conclusion of the above argument? (*1 KU*)

e) Do you think this argument is a reliable argument? Give reasons for your answer (*4 AE*)

Total: 10 Marks

Higher Critical Thinking Practice Assessment

1.   Answer the questions that follow each passage.

"Why do I think you should marry Jack? Well Jack is a fireman and all firemen are kind and well paid. So you should marry him. Don't let him get away!"

---

a)   Which sentences in this argument are statements and which are not? *(2 AE)*

b)   Identify one premise and one conclusion in the above argument. *(2 KU)*

c)   What is a 'hidden' premise? *(1 KU)*

d)   Suggest 2 possible hidden premises assumed by this argument. *(2 AE)*

e)   Is this argument inductive or deductive? Explain your answer. *(2 KU/2AE)*

"Dear Friend, a man who has studied law to its highest degree is a brilliant lawyer, for a brilliant lawyer has studied law to its highest degree."

Oscar Wilde

---

f)   Identify the premise and conclusion of this argument. *(1 KU)*

g)   What is a 'formal' fallacy? Illustrate your answer with an example. *(2 KU)*

h)   Identify the fallacy being committed in the above passage and explain why this argument is an example of this sort of fallacy. *(2 AE)*

i)   Is the above argument valid? Give a reason for your answer. *(1 KU/1 AE)*

j)   What would make the above argument sound? *(1 KU/1 AE)*

Total: 20 Marks

Answers to Practice Assessments

Answers to Intermediate 2 Critical Thinking Practice Assessment

1.

  a) What is an argument? (*1 KU*)

  - *An argument is a collection of statements put forward in support of a conclusion. In a good argument the conclusion has been drawn from the premises.*

  b) What is the difference between a statement and an argument? (*2KU*)

  - *A statement is a single sentence capable of being true or false. An argument is a collection of statements and can only be described as valid or invalid rather than true or false. A claim can be asserted or denied by a statement but and argument can prove or refute a claim.*

  c) What are the premises of the above argument? (*2 KU*)

  - *The premises are: 'Belief in God promotes respect for others' and 'If people didn't believe in God them society would be in a terrible state.'*

  d) What is the conclusion of the above argument? (*1 KU*)

  - *The conclusion is: 'God must exist.'*

  e) Do you think this argument is a reliable argument? Give reasons for your answer (*4 AE*)

  - *This argument is unreliable because it is possible for the premises to be true and the conclusion to be false. The argument also contains a fallacy known as the appeal to consequences fallacy. The appeal to consequences fallacy is when someone claims a statement is false because of the negative consequences of it being true. However, the consequences of a claim being true are often irrelevant to the issue of whether the claim is true or not. In this example the fact that society would be in a terrible state might not be relevant to the issue of whether God exists or not.*

Answers to Higher Critical Thinking Practice Assessment

1.

    a)   Which sentences in this argument are statements and which are not? *(2 AE)*

- *The statements are: 'Jack is a fireman'; 'all firemen are kind and well paid';*
  'you should marry him.' The non-statements are: 'Why do you think I should
  marry Jack?' (a question) and 'Don't let him get away!' (a command).

    b)   Identify one premise and one conclusion in the above argument. *(2 KU)*

- *The premises are: 'Jack is a fireman'; 'all firemen are kind and well paid.'*
  The conclusion is: 'You should marry him.'

    c)   What is a 'hidden' premise? *(1 KU)*

- *A hidden premise is an unstated premise which an argument nonetheless*
  assumes for its validity.

    d)   Suggest 2 possible hidden premises assumed by this argument. *(2 AE)*

- *Two possible hidden premises might be: 'You should marry people who are*
  kind and well paid' and 'Jack is kind and well paid.'

    e)   Is this argument inductive or deductive? Explain your answer. *(2 KU/2AE)*

- *The argument is deductive. Deductive arguments derive a particular*
  premise from an assumed universal conclusion. This argument does exactly
  that by beginning with a fact about all firemen and then deriving the same
  fact about a particular fireman, Jack.

    f)   Identify the premise and conclusion of this argument. *(1 KU)*

- *The premise is: 'a brilliant lawyer has studied law to its highest degree' and*
  the conclusion is: 'a man who has studied law to its highest degree is a
  brilliant lawyer.'

g)   What is a 'formal' fallacy? Illustrate your answer with an example. *(2 KU)*

- *A formal fallacy is an argument that is fallacious purely because it has an invalid form. For example, denying the antecedent is a formal fallacy because it has the invalid form: If P then Q. Not P, therefore not Q'.*

h)   Identify the fallacy being committed in the above passage and explain why this argument is an example of this sort of fallacy. *(2 AE)*

- *The fallacy in this passage is a type of circular argument. This argument is circular because the conclusion is ultimately assumed by the premise; they are ultimately the same statement. This might not seem the case at first sight since the conclusion seems to reverse the content of the premise. However, If 'a brilliant lawyer' is 'someone who has studied law to its highest degree' then these two terms are synonymous and therefore the premise and the conclusion both have the same form: 'A is A'.*

i)   Is the above argument valid? Give a reason for your answer. *(1 KU/1 AE)*

- *Valid arguments guarantee a true conclusion whenever the premises are true. Circular arguments are usually valid because if the premises are true then the conclusion must be true. In this case the premise and the conclusion are the same statement so the argument must be valid.*

j)   What would make the above argument sound? *(1 KU/1 AE)*

- *A sound argument is one which is valid and has true premises. So since the argument is valid it would be sound if it were true that 'a brilliant lawyer is someone who has studied law to its highest degree.'*

Glossary of Key Terms

The emboldened words throughout this book refer to the glossary of key terms given below. This glossary contains 100 key terms that you should be familiar with once you have completed an introductory course on Critical Thinking. As a revision exercise you could get someone else to quiz you on some randomly chosen logical terms from this list.

Ad hominem argument: Any fallacious argument which attempts to reject a claim by casting doubt on the character or credentials of the person who supports it.

Ad hominem abusive: A type of *ad hominem* argument which attacks the character that alleges some improper connection between the circumstances of the opponent and the views they support.

Ad hominem circumstantial: A type of *ad hominem* argument which alleges that the opponent stands to benefit in some way from the views that they support.

Ad hominem tu quoque: A type of *ad hominem* argument which alleges that the opponent doesn't practice what they preach.

Affirming the antecedent: A type of valid argument which has the form 'If P then Q. P, therefore Q'. Also known as *modus ponens*.

Affirming the consequent: A type of invalid argument which has the form 'If P then Q. Q, therefore P'.

Appeal to authority: A type of argument, sometimes fallacious, which supports its conclusion by reference to an eminent source.

Appeal to consequences: A type of fallacious argument which assumes that a claim is false because of the negative consequences of supporting the claim. Also known as *argumentum ad consequentiam*.

Argument: A collection of statements comprising premises and conclusions.

Argument diagrams: An informal technique for showing how the premises support the conclusion of an argument.

Argument from ignorance: A fallacious argument which assumes that a proposition is false because of lack of evidence to the contrary. See also *argumentum ad ignorantiam*.

Argumentum ad auctoritatem: A Latin name for the illegitimate appeal to authority fallacy. Also known as *argumentum ad verecundiam*.

Argumentum ad consequentiam: The Latin name for the appeal to consequences fallacy.

***Argumentum ad hominem*:** See *ad hominem argument*.

***Argumentum ad ignorantiam*:** A Latin name for the argument from ignorance fallacy.

***Argumentum ad verecundiam*:** A Latin name for the illegitimate appeal to authority fallacy. Also known as *argumentum ad auctoritatem*.

Aristotle (384-322 BC): An ancient Greek philosopher tutored by Plato, who became tutor to Alexander the Great, and the inventor of syllogistic logic.

Assert: To put forward a claim without support.

Assumed premise: An unstated premise which an argument may depend on for its validity.

Attacking the person: Any fallacious argument which attempts to reject a claim by casting doubt on the character or credentials of the person who supports it.

Begging the question: A less common name for circular reasoning.

Certain: To be known without doubt. Incapable of being false.

Circular argument/circular reasoning: An argument which assumes the truth of the conclusion in one of its premises. Usually considered to be fallacious.

Coincidental correlation: A fallacious argument which assumes that because two events are correlated in time or space that they must be causally connected in some way. Also known as *post hoc ergo propter hoc*.

Conclusion: The central claim of an argument which the premises support.

Conjunctions: Any 'and' statement such as 'I like bread and I like butter.'

Constants: Connective words in an argument form such as 'and', 'or' or 'not'.

Content: The subject matter of an argument.

Counterintuitive: To be contrary to your intuition: to go against what intuition would lead you to expect.

Declarative sentences: Another name for statements. Sentences which make a claim about the world.

Deductive arguments: Any arguments which derive a conclusion from assumed premises using reason rather than observation.

Deny: To reject without supporting reasons.

Denying the antecedent: A type of invalid argument which has the form 'If P then Q. Not P, therefore not Q'.

Denying the consequent: A type of valid argument which has the form 'If P then Q. Not Q, therefore not P'. Also known as *modus tollens*.

Disjunctions: Any 'or' statement such as 'He either had brown hair or he had black hair.'

Drawn: To be derived or deduced from.

Equivocation: A fallacy which trades on the double meaning of a word or phrase.

Establish: To support a claim with reasons.

Exclamatory sentences: Another name for exclamations such as 'Yippee!'

Exclusive use of 'or': The use of 'or' in the sense of 'one or the other but not both.'

Fallacy: An error in reason contained within an argument.

False: To be contrary to fact. Not true.

False dilemma: A type of fallacious argument which alleges that there are only two options available in a given situation when others might be available.

Form: The underlying structure of an argument.

Formal fallacy: An argument which is fallacious because it has an invalid form.

Formal methods: Recognised techniques which are used in formal logic to analyse arguments and evaluate argument validity.

Hidden premise: An unstated premise which an argument may depend on for its validity.

Illegitimate appeal to authority: Any fallacious argument which supports its conclusion by reference to an inappropriate source. Also known as *argumentum ad verecundiam* or *argumentum ad verecundiam*.

Imperative sentences: Another name for commands such as 'Get out!'

Implications: Another name for 'if/then' statements such as 'if you want to lose weight then you'll need to exercise.'

Inclusive use of 'or': The use of 'or' in the sense of 'one or the other or both.'

Indicator words: Words which signify whether a statement is intended as a premise or a conclusion such as 'because' or 'therefore'.

Inductive argument: An argument based on premises based on limited observations or experiences.

Inferred: To be derived or deduced from prior premises.

Informal fallacies: An argument which may be valid but is fallacious because of its use of false or irrelevant premises.

Informal methods: Inexact methods used in critical thinking to analyse arguments and evaluate argument validity.

Interrogative sentences: Another name for questions such as 'Do you like tea?'

Intuition: The instinct for grasping the truth without recourse to reasoning.

Invalid argument: A badly structured argument which does not guarantee a true conclusion when the premises are true.

John Venn (1834-1923): A 19th century British logician and mathematician who invented Venn diagrams.

Logic: The formal study of arguments and their forms.

*Modus ponens***:** The Latin name for affirming the antecedent.

*Modus tollens***:** The Latin name for denying the consequent.

Negations: Another name for 'not' statements such as 'I am not a football fan.'

*Non causa pro causa***:** A Latin term used to describe fallacious arguments which attribute a false cause to an event.

Ordinary language argument: An argument expressed in everyday speech.

Organon: Aristotle's system of logic which uses rules of reasoning to acquire knowledge.

*Petitio principii***:** The Latin name for circular reasoning.

*Post hoc ergo propter hoc***:** The Latin name for the fallacy of coincidental correlation.

Predicate logic: A system of logic, developed from propositional logic, which uses symbols to express the internal structure of propositions.

Predicate logic forms: Argument structures which use special symbols to represent quantifiers, subjects and predicates within an argument.

Premise: A statement in an argument that offers support for the conclusion.

Probable: To possess a degree of likelihood without being certain.

Problem of induction: The problem, highlighted by David Hume, that statements justified by empirical experience can only ever be probable, not certain.

Proposition: Another name for a statement.

Propositional logic: Another name for statement logic.

Prove: To establish a claim with supporting reasons.

Refute: To reject a claim for stated reasons.

Reliable: An argument which is valid and sound and contains no fallacies.

Rhetorical question: A question that is not intended to be answered because the answer is plainly obvious.

Set logic: A system of logic which describes relationships between statements in an argument.

Set logic forms: Argument structures which use the variables A, B and C to represent sets within an argument.

Slippery slope argument/fallacy: An argument, often fallacious, which arrives at a surprising conclusion by a series of incremental steps.

Sound argument: An argument with a valid form and true premises.

Statement: A sentence capable of being true or false. Also known as a proposition.

Statement logic: A system of logic which describes relationships between statements in an argument.

Statement logic forms: Argument structures which use the variables P, Q and R to represent component statements.

Strong/strength: Of inductive arguments to be supported by good inductive evidence.

Suppressed premise: Another name for a hidden or unstated premise.

Syllogism: A three line argument popularised by Aristotle.

Tild: The symbol '~' which is used in formal logic to represent the word 'not'.

True: To be in accordance with fact. Not false.

Truth table: A formal method for testing the validity of statement logic forms.

Unreliable argument: An argument that is either invalid or unsound or contains a fallacy.

Unsound argument: An argument which is either invalid or has a false premise or both.

Valid argument: A well structured argument which guarantees a true conclusion whenever the premises are true.

Variables: Placeholder in an argument form which can be substituted with any word or phrase.

Venn diagram: A formal method for testing the validity of set logic forms.

Weak/weakness: Of inductive arguments to be supported by poor inductive evidence.

Vel: The symbol 'v' which is used in formal logic to represent the inclusive use of 'or'.

Index